Dear ELIANE,

Joy & Success!

BUSINESS BUILDING
STRATEGIES
FROM
FRONTLINE
ENTREPRENEURS

Published by CelebrityPress™, Orlando, FL
A division of The Celebrity Branding Agency®

Celebrity Branding® is a registered trademark
Printed in the United States of America.

ISBN: 9780985714321
LCCN: 2012941314

This publication is designed to provide accurate and authoritative information with regard to the subject matter covered. It is sold with the understanding that the publisher is not engaged in rendering legal, accounting, or other professional advice. If legal advice or other expert assistance is required, the services of a competent professional should be sought. The opinions expressed by the authors in this book are not endorsed by CelebrityPress™ and are the sole responsibility of the author rendering the opinion.

Most CelebrityPress™ titles are available at special quantity discounts for bulk purchases for sales promotions, premiums, fundraising, and educational use. Special versions or book excerpts can also be created to fit specific needs.

For more information, please write:

CelebrityPress™

520 N. Orlando Ave, #2
Winter Park, FL 32789
or call 1.877.261.4930

Visit us online at www.CelebrityPressPublishing.com

OUT FRONT

BUSINESS BUILDING

★★★★★★★★★★★★★★★★★★★★★★★

STRATEGIES

—FROM—

FRONTLINE

★★★★ ENTREPRENEURS ★★★★

TABLE OF CONTENTS

CHAPTER 1

THE ART OF CLOSING THE DEAL

BY AARON RIAN

A lot of people think that, in the real estate industry, our primary job is buying and selling houses – or *helping* people buy and sell houses.

And it's true. In the five years I've spent in the real estate business here in Portland, Oregon, I've helped buy and sell a lot of houses. I own a real estate team affiliated with Keller Williams that specializes in high-end residential real estate, and my staff of 13 and I typically sell 199 houses in a year. This comes close to four houses a week.

Still, saying that we *just* buy and sell houses is missing the bigger picture.

In reality, real estate – or succeeding in real estate – is all about negotiation.

I truly believe that my job as a Realtor is to fight as hard as I can for my clients and to get them the best possible deal. At the same time, I also need to fight just as hard to convince the parties on the other side of the negotiation that they, too, are getting the best possible deal. This might sound difficult, or even impossible. But for a successful real estate agent, it's just part of the job.

And for me, it's what makes the job so rewarding, both personally and professionally.

BORN TO NEGOTIATE

Some kids are born athletes, or comedians, or storytellers. In my case, you could say I was a born negotiator. One of my earliest memories from childhood is my lemonade stand; my uncle helped me build it out of wood, and we set it up right in front of my parents' house. My sister and I would stand there all day, selling lemonade to the kids riding their bikes up and down the street and to people out walking – basically to anyone who would pass by us.

Now, most kids operate a lemonade stand like this – they make the lemonade, they set their price, they sell it for that price, and they feel like they've accomplished whatever they set out to do. Well, for me, it was a little different.

For me, the challenge wasn't just selling the lemonade; it

was seeing how much money I could get the neighborhood kids to pay for my lemonade. So, when it was really hot, or when I could tell the kids were really thirsty and desperate for something to drink, I would try to jack up the price. Or, if we sold out fast and we had been selling the lemonade for 60 cents a cup, we'd go in the house and make a new sign. And the next day, the price for a cup of our lemonade was now up to 75 cents.

When it came to the art of negotiation, I didn't stop at lemonade either. Every time one of my parents' friends came over, I would hit them up and ask, "Hey, what do you need done around your house? What kind of service do you need? Do you need your lawn mowed, can I clean out your garage, can I sweep your driveway?"

Whatever they might need, whoever the person was, I would always hit them up to see if I could make some extra money. My mom would just laugh – she thought it was funny. But she also saw the potential. I must have been only around seven years old when she told me, "You have to go into some kind of sales or some kind of business when you get older. I've never seen anyone hit my friends up so much in my entire life!"

Still, asking grown-ups what kind of work they would pay me to do may have been brave, but it didn't exactly qualify as negotiation. That part came later. After I'd do a job for one of my parents' friends, the next time they came over, I'd follow up. I'd ask if they were happy with the work I did, and of course, I'd ask for the next sale and offer to do it again. When they said, "Yes, you did a really good job, of course I'd like to hire you again," I'd give 'em another price, and guess what? It would be higher!

So, you're probably not surprised that as I got older, my original plan was to go to law school and become an attorney – what better job for an expert negotiator like me? But after starting out as an investor and developer, I made the switch and wound up in real estate. And I look at my job the same way I looked at the legal field. If I were a lawyer, I would need to fight as hard as I could for my clients' rights, or freedom. In real estate, I'm fighting to get my clients the best possible deal on what is probably the biggest investment they'll ever make.

Every day when I walk in that door, I know I'm going to have a new opportunity to fight for a client.

THE ART OF NEGOTIATION

So how exactly do I do it? How do I manage to get my buyers the biggest discounts, or get my sellers the most money possible, and get everyone to agree? This is where what I call "the art of the close" really comes into play. It's all about using those negotiating skills I developed as a kid to convince the other agent, and the other party, that they're getting the fairest deal possible.

Sometimes, that requires going above and beyond what you might expect a typical real estate agent to do, and it is definitely a lot more than just "buying and selling."

For example, two months ago I closed a deal on a house for 1.3 million dollars in an exclusive Portland-area neighborhood. This isn't atypical for me – except when you look at how far I had to go to reach that closing.

When the initial offer came in, it was about $400,000 below

the listed price that my buyer wanted. $400,000 is a lot of money, and both parties were on extreme opposite ends of the spectrum with neither interested in budging. The buyer was absolutely adamant about not coming in with a higher offer. At the same time, the seller, my client, was equally unwilling to drop the price in order to come anywhere close to that buyer's original offer.

That meant it was time for me to do what I do best.

Since I was representing the seller, one of the first things I did was to gather the facts I needed to demonstrate to the buyer – on paper – the actual value of the property. I collected all the statistics and hard data we had used to value the property to come up with our asking price and sent it to the buyer's agent as proof that our asking price was fair.

At the same time, I asked the buyer's agent to show me the data to support *their* price – the price that was $400,000 lower. I said I wanted to see their numbers so that my clients could feel comfortable with the transaction and understand where the buyer was coming from and why.

While the buyer was reviewing the info I sent over, I started the next phase of the process – turning the seller's property into a "hot property." To do this, I immediately hit the phone, called every agent who had shown the house and let them know I now had an offer on the table. Nothing generates buzz on a property more than the idea that *somebody* wants it – and *you* might be able to have it!

As expected, the buzz started spreading; the other buyers who had previewed the house learned about the offer, and suddenly everybody was interested in the property and wanted to buy it!

I ended up getting my client another offer on house, at which point, I notified all parties involved that we were in a multiple offer situation on this 1.3 million dollar home. Which, of course, made the house even more desirable.

By the time I finished the negotiating process, I closed the deal on this house for $50,000 over what my clients' original asking price had been. What was going to be a no deal or a dead deal turned into a huge success and a big win for my client – because of negotiation. Of course, to pull this off, I had to be able to read the buyers, read the seller, read the agents, evaluate the situation and then use all of that information to work the hardest I could for my client.

Anything less, and I wouldn't have been doing my job.

That's another aspect of real estate that people outside the business might not understand – you have to have the kind of personality that allows you to get the most out of any situation and gives you the best chance of closing the sale. So in one situation, I might need to be Mr. Nice Guy, and in another, I may need to be an aggressive "shark." If I'm representing two clients at the same time, I may even have to shift between those two aspects of my personality on the same day! I don't mind, because over the years I've learned that adapting my personality to the people I'm dealing with gives me the best chance to close the sale.

After all, closing is what I'm there for.

THE ART OF CLOSING *YOUR* DEAL

If you want to get the most out of your real estate transaction – and by most, I mean selling for the highest price if you're a seller, or paying the lowest possible price with the most favorable terms if you're a buyer, it will all come down to the agent you choose to represent you.

So, how do you make sure your agent will close the deal you deserve? Here are a few tips that will help you find your own "closing artist."

1. Make sure the agent you choose to work with understands the current market in your area.

2. Make sure your agent is an expert negotiator who is comfortable fighting for you and doesn't just want to accept the first offer that comes in.

3. On that note, stress to your agent that you are looking for the best deal possible.

4. Look at agents with a proven track record of success. The average agent here in Oregon sells only two or three homes a year, which doesn't give them enough money to pay their bills, let alone market your property aggressively. Look for agents with a proven marketing plan, proven negotiation skills, and a proven record of closing transactions at a higher rate than just an average realtor.

For most of you reading this, a home is the largest investment you will ever make in their lifetime – you owe it to yourself to have an expert on your side. After all, if you found out you needed open heart surgery, which would you choose – the most experienced, best surgeon with a proven track record, or the new kid just out of medical school?

Or, to look at it another way, what if you were on trial for murder? Who would you want fighting for your life and your freedom – an expert lawyer who's won 59 out of 60 cases in court, or the guy who has 2 clients and hasn't been to trial for four years because he prefers to settle?

To get what you want, to get what you deserve, you need someone on your side that is both willing and able to fight for you. In fact, with 99% of the offers I get, I wind up negotiating on terms and on price to insure they're the absolute best dollars or discounts I can get for my client.

To me, an offer coming in is just the starting point. If I'm representing a seller, my job from that point forward is to make sure that I squeeze every last possible dollar out of that buyer for my client. And if I'm representing the buyer, my job is to ensure that I save my client every dime possible in that negotiation and get them the best terms in that transaction.

That's what I love about what I do. I like convincing the other party that my client's position is the right one – every single time. I feel great knowing that I did the best job possible for my client. I love the high of making the deal – you start in a situation where you just don't know where you'll end up, and then you really get in there and fight like crazy for your client.

Whether I'm selling high-end homes or lemonade, it's all about the art of the close.

ABOUT AARON

No one knows the Portland, Oregon real estate market better than Aaron Rian, and no one works harder for his clients to bring him or her the best deals, whether their goal is to buy or sell property.

Rian was born and raised in the Portland area where he continues to live to this day. His extensive firsthand knowledge of the area gives him a powerful perspective on its most advantageous real estate opportunities. This brings immense value to his clients.

That in turn has brought Rian top-level recognition for the excellence of his work. In his five-plus years as a real estate agent, Rian has been a Top One Percent Portland Metro Realtor and a Multi-Million Dollar Sales Producer. He also won back-to-back Top Real Estate Agent awards from the *Portland Monthly* magazine in 2011 and 2012, and he was recently added to the "Registry of Business Excellence™" by America's Registry of Outstanding Professionals organization.

Rian has also begun to make his mark as a thought leader in the American real estate industry. He has appeared in such national publications as *USA Today* and *The Wall Street Journal*, and was recently featured in *Top Agent Magazine*. His first book, *Out Front: The Art of Closing a Deal*, will be available on Amazon.com later this year.

Currently, Rian supervises thirteen staff members at The Rian Group and Keller Williams Realty. Rian and his team are on track to close over 199 transactions with a value of nearly 66 million dollars in volume in 2012.

In his spare time, Rian enjoys traveling and sports of all kinds. He is an avid Portland Trail Blazers and L.A. Lakers fan and provides sponsorships for local high school basketball and football programs. He attributes his competitive negotiating skills to his experience running a lemonade stand when he was six.

CHAPTER 2

USING EDUCATIONAL MARKETING TO BUILD RAPPORT, CREDIBILITY AND CRUSH OBJECTIONS

BY GREG ROLLETT

E veryone's favorite question to answer at cocktail parties, family reunions and networking gatherings is the infamous, "So, what do you do?"

Some people have it down pat. "I'm a personal injury lawyer," or "I'm a real estate agent."

Others, not so much. "I'm a writer...a blogger...and I help people manage the social web."

When we started the ProductPros, I found myself in the difficult position of trying to explain what it is that I do and how I help people in their business. Creating information products has a place at the forefront of the information marketing business, but not so much for nearly everyone else on the planet.

For prospects and potential clients, we had to take it a step further. While they understand what an information product may be, the concept of "We'll build your product for you" is lost on many people. In comes the power of using educational marketing to help paint a picture in our prospect's mind as to what we do, how it can help them, and why we are the expert, and the company they need to hire in order to get the results they desire.

Throughout our marketing campaign, we do this in a variety of ways – from live and recorded webinars, where we place an emphasis on education for 60-90 minutes, to free reports and manifestos. We also use the media to leverage their audience to share our story and our message, providing education through print, TV and online media outlets.

One such outlet that we recently used to our advantage was working with Andrew Warner and Mixergy.com. Mixergy is an online publishing company that interviews successful CEO's and entrepreneurs in an effort to help other CEO's and entrepreneurs build successful businesses. Mixergy has interviewed the likes of Tim Ferriss, Gary Vaynerchuk, the

CEO's from Kiva, Groupon, Wikipedia and more. And now, it was my turn to help out.

Our interview was focused on creating and developing information products, even if you are not a guru. The interview was actually constructed as a step-by-step system for building, recording and releasing a first information product. The interview between Andrew and I lasted about 2 hours and was the definition of using education to gain interest, trust and rapport with a community.

After the interview was aired, numerous viewers contacted me inquiring about my work. They loved the interview and the information that I shared. The interview built a bond with the audience, as they saw my face (it was a video interview), my passion and my voice. I gave them everything that I knew about the subject.

When you are free to give value to an audience, and you over-deliver through education and information, you can quickly gain control of an audience. There is something about being vulnerable that opens you up to bonding and trust. This type of educational marketing will quickly allow you to do three powerful things in your business:

1. Build Rapport With Your Audience
2. Build Unmatched Credibility With Your Audience
3. Crush Objections That Your Market Might Have about You and What Your Business Does

In the Mixergy interview, I was able to do all of these 3 things through the education I provided in the content. The results from this interview alone have translated into $15,500 in new business, from clients that had never heard of me before the interview. That is very powerful indeed.

Let's explore how you can use education in your marketing in each of these 3 areas.

BUILDING RAPPORT WITH YOUR AUDIENCE

Today, more than ever, people are constantly being hit from every angle with advertising, information, ideas and brands. New companies, solutions, advertisers and experts are popping up literally every minute. How can you not only grab their attention, but also connect with them emotionally, making them remember you and take the next step or action?

This is done through rapport building. Wikipedia defines rapport as: "The relationship of two or more people who are *in sync* or *on the same wavelength* because they feel similar and/or relate well to each other."

In other words, in your marketing, you need to educate your marketplace that you know your market better than they do. You need to make them feel that you are just like them, that you understand them and that they can come to you when faced with a problem.

Education is the best way to do that. Think about your favorite teacher in grade school or high school – the one that opened your eyes on a subject. This teacher found a way to connect with you, to get past the bad feelings about class work, and actually got inside your head, got you to pay attention and take action (in that case, passing your exams).

You need to now do this in your marketing. A great example is from Chris Guillebeau and how he builds rapport at The

Art Of Nonconformity. Chris has been blogging about his life and his business since 2008. It started as a place to speak freely about his quest to travel to every country in the world before his 35th birthday. He is now only a handful of countries away from accomplishing this goal.

Along the way, Chris has built an online and offline publishing business that allows him to live his desired lifestyle of travel and creative production (books, blog posts, training programs and events). As he began to build his tribe, he needed to create a reason for people to follow him. He had an incredible story to tell and a movement that would resonate with a global audience that wanted more from their existing lives.

As the blog grew, Chris wrote his World Domination Manifesto, which explained his story, his travel ambitions and his new outlook on what work and life should be all about. The manifesto instantly connected with thousands of people from all over the world who were now hung up on every word Chris wrote. They were hungry for more.

Chris then developed a series of "Unconventional Guides," his first suite of products for this audience. Had Chris not educated his market about his mission, inspired them through his own journey and ambitions, and let them into his world – essentially building rapport with a hungry audience, they would not be so eager to buy his "Unconventional Guides," to help elevate his books to *New York Times* Best-Sellers, to purchase tickets to his sold-out annual World Domination events and use his game changing products.

The rapport he built is so strong and focuses on a 90% educational and informational strategy, and only 10% sales. The trust with his tribe is immense and is difficult to match in his marketplace.

In your business, you may not have the luxury of delivering 90% free and useful educational content, and that's okay. What you do need to do and understand is that you cannot underestimate the power of connecting emotionally with your audience and how they are feeling.

This can be a manifesto, a book, vulnerable blog posts, videos and even webinars or events where you can connect on that emotional level. That connection can be unmatched and can help you to build a loyal tribe.

BUILDING UNMATCHED CREDIBILITY WITH YOUR AUDIENCE

The second piece to educational marketing is showing your audience that you, and you alone are the sole expert that can solve their problem. You do this by educating them about your credibility in your marketplace. People today do business with people that they know, like and trust. They are buying you for *who* you are, *not what* you do.

Maybe businesses focus on the *what* part of their business – the features and benefits that make their product great. While it is important to be great at what you do, you need to spend more time educating people on *who* you are. What is your core story? What are your values? What makes people connect to you on a human level?

In building unmatched credibility, you also need to educate people on what you have done and the results you have achieved for people just like them. Remember, in building rapport, we were able to connect with people on that emotional level. Now it's time to show them that you are the right solution for them.

People really do relate to things that they are familiar with. In knowing that, be sure to showcase your media mentions, major awards that resonate with your market, high profile people and businesses you have done business with, and other accolades that would draw the attention in the brain of your target client or customer. All of this plants the seed for credibility.

Now, we want to take it to that next level and blow them away with our ability to help them get results. People pay big money for results. How can you create educational pieces that drive results for your clients? When I talk about product creation I always tell my audience that you need to make the first step very easy and actionable and that will deliver near instant results for your audience. You don't want to do, what I call the "P90X Pass Out Plan." This is where after seeing your material, or going through your program they are so exhausted or overwhelmed that they cannot go on, take action or get any results because their mind or their body has been completely shut down.

One great example of using education to build credibility and ignite action is from Ramit Sethi's *I Will Teach You To Be Rich*. I love this example because Sethi has two major objections to overcome from the moment someone see his name or visits his website. First, is his ethnicity. American society is not accustomed to seeing or hearing from a guru with his cultural background. India is not seen as a country where you would want to learn about financial information. His second major roadblock is the name of his site and business. It sounds like a "get rich quick" program, which it is far, far away from being in reality.

In order to overcome these obstacles, Seithi created an amazing educational series that viewers can receive right from the homepage of his website. When you visit his homepage, you will see references to major media he has been featured within and also a note about his *New York Times* best-selling book. This is an instant credibility booster. Then, instead of a traditional free report, which many people relate to *give me your email address, and I will send you a bunch of promotional e-mails to buy my stuff,* Seithi is actually giving away the kitchen sink and then some. When you opt-in to his newsletter you instantly receive content that is better than many expert or guru's paid content. It includes:

- The 80/20 Guide to Finding a Job You Love,
- The 30-day Hustling Course with interviews, worksheets and exercises
- The Idea Generator PDF and MP3
- Successful Client and Student Case Studies,
- The first chapter of his NYT best-selling book and more…

…all of this just to get an email address. That is very impressive and one look into the material and the credibility factor for what he does and teaches goes through the roof!

In your business, look for ways to over deliver and drive results for your clients before you ask them for money. Showcase your credibility in a way that helps them to accomplish their needs and desires in life and business. Once you do this, the selling becomes superfluous.

CRUSHING PROSPECT OBJECTIONS

You can use education to advance the conversation in the head of your prospect to move them one, or multiple steps closer to choosing you as the person to help them solve their problem. You have seen that with the first two steps, building rapport and building credibility. Even if you get through both of these detectors in the brains of your market, they will still have objections and red flags floating around in their minds. This is where the third and final piece of the puzzle comes together.

Everyday you hear objections as to why people are not yet ready to buy your products or services. Maybe it is price or that they don't fully understand your offer. Maybe something is conflicting in their mind, or they feel they don't have enough time to put it into play. No matter their objective, you have the ability to educate them on why their objective is not the answer and that your solution is.

Having an objection to a product or service that your market needs really means that they don't have the right education as to how it will impact their life. Your job is to educate them by teaching strategic points that paint a vivid picture in their minds that you are the right man (or woman) for the job.

If you have gotten this far, I want you to spend a few moments writing down every objection that you have heard as to why someone is not committing to your product or service. Talk to team members, write things down on a white board or just make a list on a sheet of notebook paper.

Now think about stories, case studies and information that will help to overcome each of these objections. What does your customer *not know* that is causing them to say "Not right now"?

A great example of overcoming objections in action is from Celebrity Press Publishing (CPP). Nick and his team put together a list of reasons people might not be using their publishing company. He turned those objections, or reasons, into a stellar report called "The New Rules of Becoming an Author – The 7 Myths Of Publishing Success." When someone wants to learn more or raising one of the key points mentioned in the report, the team at CPP can instantly send over the report as a PDF or mail a physical copy via FedEx that they can see, feel and read to overcome the objections that they might be having in their minds.

Nick is using educational marketing to showcase his expertise and build rapport with the audience. He showcases his credibility by telling stories of successful authors and then crushing objections. This becomes a powerful sales piece that is used as marketing. Again, it allows the prospect to come up with their own conclusion that Nick and Celebrity Press is the right solution to help their business.

THE POWER OF EDUCATIONAL MARKETING

I hope you can see how powerful using education can be in your business. It allows others to make up their minds about what you do and how you can help them. Even better is that you get to create the message and the materials. You control the output.

And if anyone ever asks you again at a party or event what you *do*, you will now be able to educate them and help them understand who you are and what you do.

ABOUT GREG

Greg Rollett, the ProductPro, is a best-selling author and online marketing expert who works with authors, experts, entertainers, entrepreneurs and business owners all over the world to help them share their knowledge and change the lives and businesses of others. After creating a successful string of his own educational products, Greg began helping others in the production and marketing of their own products.

Greg is a front-runner in utilizing the power of social media, direct response marketing and customer education to drive new leads and convert those leads into long-standing customers and advocates.

Previous clients include Coca-Cola, Miller Lite, Warner Bros and Cash Money Records, as well as hundreds of entrepreneurs and small-business owners. Greg's work has been featured on FOX News, ABC, and the Daily Buzz. Greg has written for Mashable, the Huffington Post, AOL, AMEX's Open Forum and more.

Greg loves to challenge the current business environments that constrain people to working 12-hour days during the best portions of their lives. By teaching them to leverage technology and the power of information, Greg loves helping others create freedom businesses that allow them to generate income, make the world a better place and live a radically ambitious lifestyle in the process.

A former touring musician, Greg is highly sought after as a speaker, having appeared on stages with former Florida Gov. Charlie Crist, best-selling authors Chris Brogan and Nick Nanton, as well as at events such as Affiliate Summit.

If you would like to learn more about Greg and how he can help your business, please contact him directly at greg@productprosystems.com or by calling his office at 877.897.4611.

You can also download a free report on how to create your own educational products at www.productprosystems.com.

CHAPTER 3

HOW TO GET YOUR BUSINESS OUT FRONT

BY ANDREW LOCK

With so many products competing for our attention, why is that some of them manage to stand out from the crowd, whereas others die a slow painful death, and eventually slip into oblivion? What is it that puts a product out front? What's the secret?

Marketing.

There. I said it. I completely understand that's probably not the answer you were looking for. But it's a fact. A poor product with great marketing will always outsell a great product with poor marketing. That's the reality that you have to accept. I'm not suggesting for one moment that your product should be poor quality – quite the contrary. *A great product with great marketing is the ultimate winning formula.*

I can't help you create a great product, but I can help you with your marketing. I've spent years advising small business owners about how to get more people to buy their stuff. Simple marketing strategies, easily implemented consistently, that's what will put you out front.

So, let's dive right in, with 7 ways to market your business, without breaking the bank…

MARKETING METHOD #1: POST COMMENTS ON OTHER BLOGS THAT RELATE TO YOUR INDUSTRY.

This is a powerful strategy for getting potential customers to visit your website. Here's how it works. When you submit your comment on a blog, you'll be invited to include your website URL. When someone reads your comment, if they click on your name, it'll take them over to YOUR website. Pretty cool, huh?

As an example, suppose that you're in the business of selling collectible posters. First, search Google for the phrase "collectible posters blog" to find blogs in the same niche. You can also go to blog directories such as www.Technorati.com, www.AllTop.com, and www.BlogCatalog.com. Look for the most popular blogs in your niche because they draw more visitors.

Next, add an intelligent, helpful comment in response to a post (a post is simply a short article or commentary), and remember of course to include your website URL. In the future, when other readers of the blog see your comment, if they resonate with it, they'll click through to YOUR website to see what you have to offer on the subject.

Although it might be tempting to write a short sentence in your comment, remember that your comment is an opportunity to *prove* that you can provide value. That's why it's important to write something intelligent that adds to the discussion. Your aim is for visitors to the blog to read your comment and think to themselves, "This person seems interesting, I'm gonna' check out their website to find out more."

MARKETING METHOD #2: SUBMIT A WEEKLY PRESS RELEASE TO WWW.PRLOG.COM

PRLog.com is a free submission service that'll broadcast your press release all over the Internet.

The most effective press releases are those that are either (a) controversial, (b) tie in with topical news, or (c) arouse curiosity. The most common pitfall with press releases is to write them like a sales letter. That type of press release will either be rejected or not get noticed. Instead, make sure it reads like a *news* story you would read in a newspaper. Make it factual, and avoid hype.

There's a fine line between self-promotion and creating a sense of excitement, so you might need to seek feedback from trusted friends. Of course, you always want to include your website URL and phone number in every press release.

What kind of topics can be covered in a press release? Well, a press release can be written for a significant number of events. For instance, if you've just launched a new website you could send out a press release explaining how the site is useful to your customers. If you launch a new service, a press release can be an easy way to encourage the curious to come and look. If you've added a new line to your existing offerings, a press release can alert your customers and potential clients to the good news. If you've won an industry award, a press release can help to instill a greater degree of trust in your company.

Format your release in easy to read, short paragraphs. Try to tell an interesting story, with specific details. Everyone loves stories! And don't forget to tailor the writing style to your audience. A press release written for lawyers should sound different to one that's for plumbers, obviously.

You'll learn a lot by reading press releases from other businesses, especially from press releases that obtain huge exposure. Examine what they did to create the buzz.

Your headline and opening paragraph should aim to grab the reader's attention quickly. Then, try and break down your message into the common questions like:

WHO, WHERE, WHY, WHAT, WHEN AND HOW

Before releasing your release, have it proofread by someone you trust. You'll be surprised at what they pick up on, regardless of how good your writing skills are!

MARKETING METHOD #3:
PROPOSE A JOINT VENTURE PARTNERSHIP WITH OTHER COMPANIES IN YOUR NICHE

It's easy to find suitable candidates to partner with – simply do a Google search using keywords that relate to your industry, and then look at the ads on the right hand side of the page.

These paid ads prove that a company is willing to spend money promoting their product or service, so it'll be easy to persuade them to try a method of making money that doesn't require them to spend more money! Ideally, call them on the phone with your proposal (suggest that they offer your product to their customers, in return for a substantial share of the profits).

Be friendly, and emphasize the merits of your product or service.

It may take you awhile to get through to the decision maker. Be patient and persistent, without being a pain.

Here's an example of how you might format a letter to a potential joint venture partner in a local market:

Dear X,

I have a rather unusual proposition for you.

My name is {Your Name} and I'm a {your occupation} right here in {your city} since {date you opened}. During this time I've been lucky enough to serve {#} {customers/families}.

Recently, I was thinking of a way to market my {business/practice} in a cost-effective manner. I realized I could do something that would be an excellent opportunity for you to gain enormous goodwill from your {clients/customers} while we both benefit.

I am in the position to let you give away a very valuable service from me, which will greatly endear your clients to you – without costing you a dime.

Let me explain.

I would like to send a letter coming from you giving your clients a coupon for a free {product/ consultation/ service} with me. During this time, I'll {explain benefits of free gift}. This service normally costs {$xxxx}.

It would be perceived as a great thank you gift from you!

And it will not cost you anything or take any of your time. In fact, I will pay 100% of the costs involved (postage and printing etc). Plus, I'll write the entire letter for you and you can have complete editorial control of it.

Please remember, this will in no way be competitive with your services. I just reasoned it would make an excellent gift you can give away to your clients for their business and a way for me to attract more people to my {business/practice}. There are no strings attached, and your clients have no obligation to ever use my {product/services} again.

If this sounds like a good idea (and it really is), I'd be happy to give you a free {product/consultation/service}, so you can see for yourself how great this {product/service} really is.

Please call me at {xxx-xxx-xxxx}, and I'll explain everything in full detail.

Sincerely,

{Your Name}

MARKETING METHOD #4: POST CLASSIFIED ADS ON THE MANY ONLINE CLASSIFIED AD WEBSITES

A frequently overlooked method of getting traffic to your website is posting free classified ads online. Classified ad postings will attract people to your site AND provide you with many *backlinks* from these websites to yours, which will help raise the profile of your website on the natural search engine rankings.

This is an ideal task to outsource because it's repetitive (and boring) work that anyone can learn. Also, the value to your business can be substantial when you do it right.

So how does it work? Well, think of a classified ad in a newspaper. It's almost identical online, except there's another benefit in that you're generating hundreds of quality *backlinks* to your website when you put your URL in the ad.

Step 1: Register for your free account at each of the websites. It's useful to use the same login information for each one to make it easier to remember. This won't be possible for all sites, so keep a record of all the sites and logins on an excel spreadsheet (or just use a notepad and pen); keep it in a safe place.

Step 2: Prepare the ad. It should be brief and to the point. It should have an irresistible offer, a compelling reason for the reader to respond, with clear instructions on what they should do next if they're interested. Try to make it sound as natural as possible –read other ads to get an idea of how other people write their ads. Save the ad to a text file like WordPad or NotePad so you can easily copy and paste it multiple times as you visit the various sites.

Step 3: Login to the site and paste the copy from the text file when prompted to enter your ad. If you want to remember the logins for each site automatically, use RoboForm (see www.roboform.com), an inexpensive piece of software that manages all the logins.

There are some details to be aware of when posting ads...

Firstly, on some sites such as Craigslist there are numerous geographic regions to choose from. In other words, you can't post one ad that covers the entire country; it doesn't work like that. You MUST select a region in order to place the ad, so always choose the areas with the largest populations first – that way you can reach the maximum number of people. In the USA, that would be New York, Los Angeles, Chicago, San Francisco, Miami, Boston and Washington DC etc.

Be aware that under normal circumstances you're not allowed to post ads in more than one geographic area. The way to overcome this is to use a different e-mail address for each posting (register multiple free Gmail accounts). Also, vary the ad descriptions each time (change the order of the words or sentence structure).

Try to select an appropriate category when given the option.

Sometimes ads will be removed if they're not seen as a good fit for the category they're in. Finally, post ads consistently. Schedule this task every week.

Make your message brief, to the point, with a compelling reason for the prospect to respond. Ideally, offer something of value, such as a free report, audio CD, DVD etc.

MARKETING METHOD #5:
START A BLOG THAT HELPS AND EDUCATES PEOPLE RATHER THAN TRYING TO SELL

You can setup a free blog using services such as www.SquareSpace.com or www.Weebly.com. Alternatively, you can use a free web hosting service such as www.Doteasy.com, and install WordPress, a blogging platform, which is also free.

The most important key to success with a blog is to provide value to readers, rather than trying to persuade them to buy. Offer value first, build a relationship with them so that they get to know, like, and trust you, and you'll soon find that people will naturally ask what they can buy from you.

Once your blog has at least 20 posts on it, submit the URL to popular blog directories to let them know you exist. These include:

http://blogs.botw.org

http://www.blogcatalog.com

http://www.bloggeries.com

http://portal.eatonweb.com

http://www.ontoplist.com

http://www.blogged.com

http://www.globeofblogs.com

This method of marketing takes time, but it's a solid approach to building a long-term business.

MARKETING METHOD #6:
OFFER TO HELP OTHER INFLUENTIAL
BUSINESS OWNERS IN YOUR NICHE

Not only will you develop valuable relationships with people who are already successful, but there's a hidden *marketing* benefit that will occur. When you help someone else, you trigger a psychological rule called *reciprocity*. In essence, this means that when you do something good for someone, they cannot help but want to do something for you in return. It works every time. You'll feel good about helping them, and they'll feel great about helping you in return.

How specifically can you help others? Well, what skills do you have that could be of benefit to others? If you're an expert at WordPress, you could suggest some helpful plugins that would enhance the person's blog. If you're an expert writer, you could offer to write some articles to help promote their business. Use your imagination and get creative. Everyone has skills and abilities that are useful; don't take that for granted!

I know a number of people who have used this free marketing method effectively. As a result of offering assistance to others, they've become good friends with very influential business owners who have reciprocated far beyond the value of the initial help given. Again, your only commitment is time, a willingness to use your skills to help someone who might help you in the future.

MARKETING METHOD #7:
CREATE A FACEBOOK PROFILE, LINKEDIN PROFILE AND TWITTER ACCOUNT

These are the best social networking sites for business owners. Simply listing your website URL within your profile on each of these sites will give you high quality back links to your site. In addition, add your photo, a description about what your business does for others, and some personal information that makes you seem more human and likeable! Also, use these networks to network! They're great tools for making useful, profitable connections.

Never try to directly sell through these channels since you'll be viewed like the Multi-Level-Marketing *guest* at a party, who becomes a pest because they won't stop pitching their product! Be human, engage and interact with others who share similar interests and always aim to provide value to others FIRST. Do that, and they'll most likely want to reciprocate without you even asking.

Be careful with Twitter, it can suck time like a vampire. Use it sparingly to provide value to others. For example, use it to share web tools and resources you think others might find helpful or useful. Never pitch. The more value you provide others, the more they'll want to listen to you and help you.

As you can see, it's easier than you think to get out front, in any industry. Follow the blueprint laid out in this chapter, and I'll see you out front!

ABOUT ANDREW

Maverick Marketer and WebTV Expert

Andrew Lock is a maverick marketer who presents the number one WebTV show for Entrepreneurs: "Help! My Business Sucks!"

Visit: www.HelpMyBusiness.com

The free, weekly show provides plenty of practical marketing tips, big lessons from well known brands, and lots of little known resources that small business owners can use to increase their profits fast.

With an irreverent, entertaining and humorous style, the show has become more popular than a supermodel at a Catholic boarding school. Actually, it's the number one most popular marketing WebTV show in the Apple iTunes store, beating well-known traditional business training competitors like *Harvard Business Review, Advertising Age and Business Week.*

Andrew is on a mission to expose traditional marketing techniques as outdated and ineffective. You'll discover much better ways of promoting your business to make it stand out from the crowd. You'll also discover that *"marketing is everything and everything is marketing"* – a phrase that you'll hear a lot from Andrew.

Andrew's Story

It all started with potatoes...

As a kid, Andrew challenged every *normal* way of making money that was accepted by all the other kids. While most school-age youths were doing a newspaper round to earn some pocket money, Andrew hated getting up early in the morning so that option didn't seem like a good idea. Besides, he was never one to blindly follow the crowd; and he knew he could do better, regardless of his young age and inexperience.

One day, while traveling on a bus, he overheard some elderly people complain to each other about not being able to carry bags of potatoes home from the store and that sparked an idea to create a *potato round*.

Andrew found a farm that was willing to supply sacks of potatoes and had his parents drive him over to collect them. He then divided the potatoes into small *retail* bags and went from door to door, quickly establishing a little business that earned him 18-20 times more than his school friends were making with their newspaper rounds – AND he was able to do it after school, not at 5a.m. in the freezing cold of British winters.

Andrew comments, "I had no interest in potatoes, but the money was hard to pass up. Actually, I got a lot of satisfaction from helping so many people who couldn't get out of the house. They really appreciated the service and would frequently pay me more than the asking price. I realized at that point that, within reason, price sometimes isn't an issue. If demand is high and there's no competition, price is often taken out of the equation. That was one of my earliest marketing lessons at a time when I didn't even know what marketing was!"

Andrew's weekly WebTV show can be viewed at www.HelpMyBusiness.com. If you have an interest in creating your own WebTV show, grab Andrew's home study course at www.StartYourOwnTVShow.com.

CHAPTER 4

ENGLISH AS A FOREIGN LANGUAGE – FOR TECHNOLOGY PROFESSIONALS

(OR, YOU CAN BE ON THE BUS, OFF THE BUS – BUT THERE IS A BUS...)

BY DAVID WOLFE

In April of 1982, I was driving back from a company event at the Houston Open golf tournament. It was a Friday night, and the traffic was really bad. As I was sitting there in the freeway parking lot, I told myself that I was sick and tired of the Houston traffic and really missed Austin (where I had graduated from the University of Texas with an accounting degree a few years earlier). A few months later, I answered a small two-line ad in the Houston Chronicle. An Austin real estate company was looking for a Controller. What I didn't know was that the company was Barnes/Connally – a real estate development company owned by former Texas Speaker of the House Ben Barnes and former Governor of Texas John Connally.

I interviewed, made the cut, and got the job. I was 24 years old.

On my first day on the job, I got to meet Barnes. I was ushered into his office to discuss my background. He asked me how old I was. I told him. Ben, who always had a big fat cigar in his mouth, leaned over the desk and said to me:

"When I was 24, I had people who would kill for me." Well, okay…

A few months later, I had my first sit-down with 'The Governor'. I was coming in to give Connally bad news about loans that were coming due and other house-of-cards information. I was the proverbial 'Messenger'. A lot of the meeting is a blur, because I was scared shitless – but what I do remember was something he told me that he had learned from LBJ (he was Johnson's assistant in the 1940s). And it was this:

1. Answer your own phone.
2. Return all of your phone calls.
3. Speak plainly. Do not use fancy words or hide behind credentials.
4. Protect those who employ you.

SPEAK PLAINLY.
PROTECT THOSE WHO EMPLOY YOU.

My consulting firm, Lupine Partners, became a reality on February 1, 1993. Even when I was working as an accountant in the 1980s, I was always tinkering with the software programs and 'the code'. That is where my talents were – not on the accounting side of things. With the real estate knowledge I picked up working for Governors Barnes and Connally, starting this company, specializing in real estate software, was a natural fit. One of my goals was to have an organization where we didn't use *consultant-speak* – where acronyms were not allowed – in fact, forbidden – and where we "speak plainly" and "protect those who employed you" – the clients.

I spend a lot of time talking to my consulting staff about language. If they speak, and our clients don't understand what the heck they are talking about then nothing has happened. Speak plainly. Also, speak the language of the constituents – accountants, business owners, IT professionals and real estate operations professionals. It's important, and it's not easy.

In the real world, people, particularly Information Technology professionals, speak in a language that is often hard to understand. At times, it is done on purpose to confuse. It is usually done out of insecurity. We have built an entire consulting division around this pervasive business problem, and it goes something like this:

One, people start and own businesses. Two, the use and strategic implementation of technology is no longer an option for business owners. Three, entrepreneurs and technology professionals do not speak the language. Four, the technology professionals are to blame.

After being on-site for 20 years and working with hundreds (thousands?) of business owners, real estate operators, accountants, and information technology professionals, I can proudly anoint myself the nation's top *technology bartender.* Here is what the business owners tell me:

"I feel like I am hostage with my IT guy – he has the keys to the kingdom. I couldn't fire him if I wanted to."

"I am so frustrated that I cannot get a straight answer from my guy. All the acronyms – oy!"

"I feel like he is hiding things from me – I can't say exactly what it is, but something. I have no proof, just an intuitive feeling."

"I have often wondered if my technology guy is reading my private emails…"

And from the Information Technology Professionals:

"I don't know how they even started this company – I don't think they are very smart and certainly do not understand anything about technology."

"My operations guy does not care anything about keeping the technology 'current'. I want to implement the cool stuff."

"I do not at all understand why I do not get to attend the monthly strategy meetings. Everybody else at my level is there. It's not fair…"

In short, there is a lot of tension and distrust. Not in all cases – I definitely have clients where the IT professional has a seat at the strategy table and is a valued member of the team. But frankly, it is rare. A large part of our practice now is bridging the communication gap between people who own and run businesses and the professionals who are necessary to help the business owners achieve their goals.

Professionally, I wear three hats. One, I'm a business owner, and it's the main hat. Two, I am a technology consultant who has been going on-site for the past 20 years working with clients on real estate technology software evaluation and implementation projects. Three, I am a Certified Public Accountant having passed the exam in 1980 and becoming a licensed CPA in 1982. I am uniquely qualified to comment on the technology communication issue.

As a service to Information Technology professionals, I have listed below the six things you must understand about business, business owners and the business world in order to take the next step up in your career:

ONE. The main purpose of the business is to earn a profit for the owners/shareholders of the business, and to earn as high as profit as possible for as long as possible. The United States, to an extent, was founded on this capitalistic premise. To some, the American Dream is to work hard, start your own company and to control your own destiny. Most IT professionals do not understand this underlying premise. It's more of a vague concept. The purpose of the business is not to be on the cutting edge of technology. Technology is only important to the extent that it furthers the goals of the organization. It is a means, not an end. Even if you are in the business of selling technology solutions (like my company), technology in and of itself is still a means.

TWO. You must understand how a business owner thinks and understand it's a one-way street. Remember what Governor Connally said – "Protect those who employ you." There is a phrase in marketing that goes something like this: You should endeavor to enter the conversation that is going on inside the mind of your prospect. Similarly, you should be doing the same with your constituency and the people that you serve.

Listed below is a quick scattershot of what goes through my head on a recurring basis:

- How do I cover my monthly nut?
- Who is stealing from me?
- What are my upcoming marketing initiatives?
- Are my clients satisfied with the work my consultants are doing?
- Do I have any clients who may not pay me?
- What problems exist in the market
- What are good service-offering fits for my company?
- Is there competition I should be concerned with?
- Do I have any short-term cash flow issues that may affect my ability to make payroll?
- Where is the consulting talent – where can I find my next terrific consultant and make Lupine their permanent employment home?

THREE. Words matter. You've heard the line – If a tree falls in a forest and no one is around to hear it, does it make a sound? Same thing here – if a technology professional has a business conversation with another business professional and does not take the time to choose non-technical words to explain a business issue, and the receiving party does not understand what the hell the technology professional is talking about, then has anything happened? Answer: No.

If you speak in 'techno-babble', then you are not serving your employer. The reality of the matter is the technology professional has to change the way he or she speaks so 'lay' people will understand them. Profit trumps technology.

Here is a question for the technology professional: Is what you are trying to describe really that complicated? Or are you trying to act important and to confuse? You will know you have arrived when you can make the complicated simple for your peers and associates, and when you can put yourself in the shoes of your employer. See number 2 above.

FOUR. You can be on the bus, off the bus – but there *is* a bus. What I am saying here is that you can get onboard and make the required changes in yourself, or you can continue with the status quo. Once you get 'on the bus', you will begin being perceived as a valued member of the pack.

As a consultant, I have taught myself to be a trusted advisor, not an annoying pest. I bring solutions to my clients. If I am calling my clients, they know that I have something that might be of interest to them in their business. I NEVER call to pitch services. This dynamic should be your primary goal in your technology 'practice' with your employer.

Your success, to an extent, has little to do with how good you are at technology. It will be more geared towards how empathetic you are to your employer and to what it is he is trying to achieve. Linguistics will earn you more money than being a technician.

FIVE. Hiding the 'keys to the kingdom' may be harmful to your professional health. One of the dynamics I see with some of my clients is the IT professional who thinks they are guaranteeing their longevity at the company by 'hiding' access to key passwords and administrative rights. Just so you know – it really pisses people off. Yes, certainly, there are many passwords and rights that should not be shared. But... there should be somebody who has access to this information – at a minimum, the business owner. After all it is their data. They own it. At Lupine, we have a 'hit by the bus' protocol. All key functions have been filmed using a software product called Camtasia so we can stay operational in the event of personal catastrophes.

If you insist on this behavior then you will ultimately lose your job. It will be a silent coup, and you will not see it coming. I may even be hired to be your 'assassin'. Your security is making all 'secret' information accessible to certain upper echelon people in the organization. Your security is making sure the company functions if something happens to you. Your security is in being a complete tactical partner – which includes sharing the kingdom keys.

SIX. You must understand your employer's business. Get educated on the operations and accounting aspects of the business. Ask questions! I have sat through countless meetings where the IT director was clueless. On the other hand, I could count (on one hand) the number of IT professionals who could completely describe the business they were in and could confidently describe issues and problems.

If you are at a meeting and you are doing the head-nod thing and you do not have any idea of what is being discussed, then you are guilty of professional insecurity. This can be fixed. Become determined to learn as much about your employer's business as you can. Find a mentor or somebody you admire. All of us like to talk about ourselves. Ask to take them to lunch. Have your questions ready. Get the knowledge. Trust me on this: Your curiosity will be VERY well perceived.

CONFIDENTIAL BONUS FOR BUSINESS OWNERS: Lean in close, I am in whisper voice. You need to know this... Systems are your 'invisible employee'. They work 24 hours per day, 7 days per week and 365 days out of the year. They don't whine. They are chomping at the bit to go to work. They rarely ask for a raise (unless the software company increases the annual license fee), and they never go on vacation. They are also many times your most expensive 'employee'. Also, your invisible employee has a boss, and it ain't you. It's your IT professional. You need to watch their relationship carefully, as there is lots of money at stake; and the magnitude is not of the order of 'coins found in the sofa'... do not abdicate this responsibility.

CONFIDENTIAL BONUS TO TECHNOLOGY PROFESSIONALS: You really are in the marketing business...

ABOUT DAVID

David Wolfe, CPA is the Founder and President of the boutique technology consulting firm Lupine Partners. Founded in 1993, Lupine provides software evaluation and implementation services to a wide base of real estate organizations across the United States. David is the author of two other books: *Software and Vendors and Requirements, Oh My! – A Project Team's Guide to Evaluating Business Software*, and *Lessons from the Technology Front Line*. Additionally, David has served as an expert witness in court cases where data ownership was in dispute.

In his private practice, David teaches information technology professionals how to provide more value to their employers through understanding the components of business operations and accounting. Technology professionals are taught the fundamentals of business, and more importantly, the tactics of communicating with entrepreneurs – ultimately becoming Trusted Advisors in their own right.

Similarly, David advises technology-phobic business owners and other professionals on the language of technology, how to leverage technology for higher profits with less hassle and the tactics of motivating and cultivating a technology team that serves their interests.

As a sought after speaker, you can contact David at dwolfe@lupinepartners. com. Please visit the Lupine Partners website at www.lupinepartners.com/PrivatePractice.php for more information about Lupine Partners and David's private consulting practice.

CHAPTER 5

QUALITY ISN'T EXPENSIVE; IT'S PRICELESS

BY FRANK ISTUETA

We all deserve and have the opportunity to receive the best our money can buy. Most of the time, we don't take the time to educate ourselves or to look for what characteristics make a product or service better. How are we going to feel when a great service is delivered to us? How long is the product going to be performing to our expectations? How much comfort will it provide while we use it? How happy are we going to be if we know our money is well invested? When we buy a good product or service we feel respected and valued. When we can buy the best service available we feel better because we know that our time is appreciated and that we are receiving what we paid for, and sometimes even more than that.

I was born into a family of entrepreneurs; and, luckily enough, I came into this world at the same time that a communist government was beginning to control every aspect of people's lives and taking away all private properties and businesses. Everything I heard as a young child was how well things used to be. Cuba is only 90 miles from the United States, and before Castro many of the products available in Cuba wore the famous tag "Made in the USA." I remember that as pride of American industry, as a pride of products, tools, equipment, appliances, and cars that were well made. Everyone always referred to the past times as better. They would talk about the way private businesses used to deliver services, how many options they used to provide, and the many options in businesses you used to be able to choose from. I became a fanatic for everything we could no longer have, including freedom.

When I arrived to this beautiful country, my first job was as an assistant in a small handyman company providing services to high-end clientele. I learned many different trades, as well as, what the clients expected and demanded. In my young entrepreneur mind, I formed dreams; I started creating a vision of my own business in the construction industry. After various small jobs on my own, it was easy to realize the market was thirsting for quality, and not only for a complete product, but also for every aspect of what makes a service business a top notch business.

The circumstances were this: I was new to this wonderful country; I had no budget, and I had very little money; but I had a big American dream to become successful and that put me on the right path. At the beginning, I used to do everything including the *marketing*. I used to do canvassing and hand out flyers. I used to answer the phone, produce the jobs (whenever there was one), order the materials, dispose of the garbage. Yes, I did almost everything. I count it all as a blessing. I learned all the parts of the business. Almost all of us entrepreneurs go through this unless there is a sufficient budget to do it differently.

All we need are big dreams, big goals and the right environment. I'm living my dream in the country that is known for the best products, the best services and the best negotiators. If we want to go somewhere or do something, there is a strong possibility somebody is already there or has done it before. I became an observer and a strongly dedicated student and reader of every bit of information that could make my dreams a reality.

Then I started to get lucky (when preparation meets opportunities). I married the right woman that complimented my dreams and supported me. My business relations began to grow. And finally, all the components started to come into place. The first clients we had were happy and started to refer us to their family and friends. We started to get better in everything that we delivered, and most importantly, every person that joined our new small and growing company set out to be the best.

In any successful business or organization, the commitment to customer service always begins at the top. The company's leaders must buy into the fact that they not only need to meet their customer's expectations, but they must strive to exceed them. They must develop a company culture that understands, embraces and executes this concept.

In today's world, business competition is tougher than ever. If you can't provide goods or services when somebody wants or needs them, there are often four or five other companies immediately ready to fill this void. You only get one chance to make a good first impression. If the company's leaders do not accept this fact or are not willing to provide the necessary resources to meet their customer's needs, they will soon find themselves scrambling for business.

Proper training is one way to develop a company culture that embraces excellent customer service. Every employee in the company must understand implicitly what is expected of them when interacting with customers. Is there an established, uniform way to answer the phone? Are there set procedures in place for instances when a customer has a question or problem? Is there an established chain of command to make sure that issues are handled in a timely fashion? And most importantly is everyone trained to carry out these company procedures?

It all comes down to one word: "Wow!" Customer service is not a superficial covering that a business puts on to make itself more appealing to potential clients, but something that is generated from its very core. If you tell your employees to smile and you don't back up everything that you do with that consistent message, it won't work.

You want to *wow* your customers, and you need to create an environment to support that goal. Providing a consistent message that lets your employees know why customer service is important is essential. Providing realistic tasks with achievable goals is an important way to communicate respect for your employees that creates a supportive customer service environment.

Remember – how you handle a problem is far more important than the problem itself. A customer must always be made to know that their best interests are being given serious consideration, even when you can't give in to their demands.

So, everything else being equal, why is it that some companies thrive in the face of adversity, while others fall apart? Studies have shown that it is not because a company offers a lower price, or even a better product or service, for that matter. The truth is that customers prefer to spend their money with companies that give them the attention they feel they deserve.

Today, having a "satisfied customer" is not enough; what you want is a customer who is going to tell everyone they know about you and your company. Many times we just assume that because they gave us the final check all is fine… not so. You want to know for sure, because the experience they had with you is what they're going to tell the world.

A happy client is a pleasure to have, but an ecstatic one is even better. When you go above-and-beyond to *wow* your clients, they can become a wellspring of repeat business. They'll refer new customers to you, and publicly reinforce your reputation to others over and over again.

But how do you turn an ordinary client into a raving fan? All it takes is a little understanding of their wants and needs – and some creative strategies for exceeding their expectations. Here are 10 ways to create raving clients who provide the word-of-mouth marketing that your business needs to succeed.

1. **Identify service motivation and mission.** Customer service employees can best serve customers when they recognize their own passions and apply them to their line of work.

2. **Define great service for your organization.** Businesses can wow customers through customer service add-ons, and staples like honesty and efficiency are always effective.

3. **Form great relationships.** Relationships are built on reciprocity, so customer service staff should be willing to give value and gifts to make up for customer issues.

4. **Build trusting relationships that last.** Trust is variable, but companies can build connections with customers through listening well and asking in-depth questions.

5. **Be positive.** Customer service members should use cheerful and positive language to avoid negative situations with customers before they begin.

6. **Aggressively solve problems—the bigger the better.** Staff members give excellent service when they are able to understand a problem, research it, and offer customers several different solutions.

7. **Recover from mistakes gracefully.** Mistakes will occur, but skilled customer service representatives are able to apologize to the customer no matter what went wrong and repair the damage caused.

8. **Give customers and yourself a break.** People have different types of personalities and different ways of learning. Service staff should be able to change tactics based on the personality of the customer.

9. **Keep it cool when things get hot**. Angry customers are difficult to deal with, but customer service members should respond with assertiveness and empathy.

10. **Be your own best customer.** The best customer service employees take care of themselves as much as they take care of customers.

Don't over-promise – be realistic and focused when telling them what you'll deliver and when they should expect it. Then go the extra mile to make your deliverable impressive and on time (or better yet, early). This is simply the easiest way to secure your reputation – the very currency of marketing itself. It virtually guarantees a stream of revenue from your current clients and the clients they refer to you in the future.

Make sure your customers know that they are always welcome to call you if there is a problem. Any time you complete a project, you should call the customer to follow-up after the work is completed. People want to know that they are being taken care of – and it's not just follow-up calls that are important, but timely follow-ups.

It's often said that happy customers will tell four people about their experience with a business. On the other hand, an unhappy customer will tell ten people of their negative experience with a business. Positive word of mouth marketing is one of the best methods of advertising. When a relative or friend states that they had exceptional service at a particular company, there's a better than average chance that the recipient of this positive statement will patronize the establishment.

One of the goals of any organization should be to assemble the best team of people and professionals in the market. Everyone on the team should be committed to providing the best experience for the clients. The client is the one that keeps the company running, and the client is the one that pays everyone's salary in the company. They are the *real bosses* and every employee in the company must be aware of this.

Our commitment and the quality work that we deliver have paid off. We have been honored to receive awards for being on the "Top 200 Remodelers" list since 2005, and recently we have been selected for the prestigious BIG 50 by *Remodeling Magazine.* Each year, *Remodeling* editors interview people from the nominated companies and often talk to competitors, suppliers, and subcontractors. Also weighing into the decision are multiple nominations for a single company, geography, longevity, profitability and best practice standards. After the research is finished, the *Remodeling* editors select the top 50 remodelers who exemplify the very best in the industry that year and who have something to offer other remodelers in proven practices. The winners are put in some or all of the following categories:

- **Business Savvy:** Remodelers with especially effective, established business systems.

- **Fine Design:** Remodelers with high aesthetic standards for their projects.

- **Industry Impact:** Remodelers who have taken active leadership roles in industry-building activities.

- **Market Wise:** Remodelers who have built their business around a keen understanding of their markets.

- **Movers & Shakers:** Owners of larger remodeling

companies that aggressively expand market share while maintaining service standards.

- **Niches:** Remodelers who have built successful companies serving an easily overlooked but profitable corner of the market.

- **Sales & Marketing:** Remodelers with effective systems for obtaining leads and closing sales.

- **Teamwork:** Owners of remodeling companies whose personnel work together effectively to achieve more than the sum of their individual work.

We are one of the proud Big 50 in 2012 and that is a product of the fine organization that we have created, and it's the result of every team member providing their best in their daily work.

I'd like to share with you some of the testimonials we have received from our satisfied clients on a regular basis.

"I want to personally thank you for the job performed by your company on the roof replacement for my house in Miami Beach. Your team was truly excellent: from Sales (Richard) to installation (Danny) and all the individual employees. Not only was your team very knowledgeable, but they also were punctual, detail-oriented and they cleaned up all the debris daily. The quality of the product and workmanship were excellent, the job was performed in a timely manner and the price was fair. It is rare to find a quality organization in the South Florida construction market, so I congratulate you and wish you the best of luck with continued success. It is easy to see why you have had a successful business for so many years. Keep up the good work. I am happy to recom-

mend Istueta Roofing to anyone who asks."

"Thank you for great service, beginning with the estimate (Omar) to the repair and follow up (Manny). I will recommend your business to everyone. You are very professional and your employees are a pleasure to work with.

Thank You,

Patty"

"We have successfully for many years done business with Istueta Roofing. Istueta Roofing has proven time and time again to be one of the highest-caliber organizations in the South Florida home improvement market. We have recommended Istueta Roofing to others because of our satisfaction with their excellent workmanship. We look forward to a continued friendly and professional business relationship with Istueta Roofing."

We are constantly looking for ways to do things better and to continually improve. We take a combined 200 plus hours of seminars and training throughout the year. Our client representatives have a weekly meeting in order to refresh and stay focused on the objective of the high quality service that we provide, and our production team meets every two weeks for what we call TQM (total quality meeting). All of this preparation and training allows our team to provide the clients what they deserve...the best quality service and the best quality product.

In closing, I want to say thank you to every member of our team, to Certified Contractors Network for their support, educational training and guidance, and for the invaluable sharing of knowledge from every member of CCN. I also want to thank my wife and family and every client that insists on the best, that respects their valuable time, that educates themselves about what they want and knows how to invest properly in invaluable services and invaluable products.

"Quality isn't Expensive...its Priceless"

TIPS FOR AN OUTSTANDING SERVICE:

- Know who your customers are and what they want. Ask them, and they will tell you.

- Train your people and treat them well; they will treat the client the way they are treated by you. *There is no way that the quality of customer service can exceed the quality of the people who provide that service.*

- Build your business on customer loyalty. This is only achieved by delivering exceptional customer service.

- Listen to your clients and keep your promises.

- You will almost always have a complaint. Resolve the issue professionally and with a win-win resolution. Complaints are an opportunity to get better and to show your commitment to quality.

- Set goals and have a clear and detailed vision of where you want to position your business.

ABOUT FRANK

Frank Istueta has 27 years of experience in the construction service industry. He started as a handyman and learned different trades in construction and always had a big dream of creating his own company. He became an entrepreneur and started his dream by creating Istueta Roofing in 1985 to provide roofing services in Miami, Florida.

Frank first began serving clients whose homes were in need of roofing repair work. Due to his personal service and unmatched vision for quality, the company continues to grow to this day and is considered and labeled by clients as "The Most Trusted Roofer in South Florida."

Istueta Roofing has won many awards in the remodeling business, including the Top 500 Re-modeler Award for the years 2005-2010, Top 200 Exterior Contractors in the nation from 2007-2011, and also the Top Roofing Contractor Award for the year 2008, as published in the *South Florida Business Journal.*

Frank was recently inducted into the *Remodeling* Big 50 class of 2012, becoming one of only 50 re-modelers in the nation to receive this honor in the year 2012.

Many of his team members at Istueta Roofing have been honored in previous years with awards from Certified Contractors Network, and they've also collected hundreds of valuable testimonials from happy clients through the years because of unparalleled service.

Servicing the most prestigious communities with thousands of completed projects produced satisfied clients in Miami, Grand Cayman, Puerto Rico, and Turks and Caicos. Frank has become an authority in the roofing business and the remodeling industry. His company provides a large range of services closely related to roofing such as, waterproofing, gutters, painting, coatings, architectural metal and a unique Platinum Client Maintenance Program for selected clientele.

Frank is married to his wife of 26 years, Leticia. They have two sons and a daughter.

To learn more about Istueta Roofing visit www.istuetaroofing.com. From there, you can follow links to Facebook, Twitter and LinkedIn accounts.

You can also follow the company on YouTube at www.youtube.com/Istueta

CHAPTER 6

BUST YOUR BELIEFS TO WIN

BY BARBARA COOPER

The locker room was full of noise and bustle, and I was determined to remain quiet and uninvolved. The nerves were kicking in, even though I still had two hours before the match. I knew how important this game was. My sports psychologist and I had been preparing for this for 12 months. Any final is always a big deal, but this was the World Masters and my opponent was a fellow international player who had represented Australia when I had played for Great Britain on the World professional squash circuit.

I knew her style, tenacity and Australian competitiveness.

Her swing was flat and low, taking more room than most, which meant I needed to be prepared to get hit or give her way too much room to play the ball. Either way, I was going to have to work for the win.

I started my warm-up routine feeling the butterflies in my stomach. As a competitive athlete with decades of international experience, I would have been more worried had I not felt nervous. I visualized my game plan – making the game long and hard. I was going to wear her down. I had the fitness to do it.

My coach and I went through our checklist of what to expect, and I was ready. My game plan was locked into my brain, my body was warmed up and loose, my rackets all had new grips – let the games begin!

What a shock! I stuck to my game plan, but was losing. The first game came and went. I left the court to get water and ask for guidance, and my coach said to hit the ball short to the front of the court. I could not believe it, let alone do it! That felt like a crazy idea, and it went against my prepared game plan. "No, that couldn't be the solution," I said to myself. I believed the way I played the first game was eventually going to work, and I would win. Playing short drop shots was far too risky. I was sure it was not the answer.

On I slogged through game two with the outstanding reward of also losing that game. I believe it was Einstein who said that doing the same thing, expecting a different result, was the definition of insanity. I was truly insane! My beliefs had me locked into this crazy scenario and ineffective game plan. Game two came and went, and now I was in a situation where my opponent only had to win a third game to collect the trophy and the World Masters Title – not a happy thought for me. Out of the court I walked at the end of this second game and again my coach was nearly screaming at me to drop the ball short. She was begging me to stop playing all those lovely deep shots and to change it up. I was not hearing the instructions. They were literally going in one ear and out the other. I did not feel confident enough to completely change the game plan in which I had so much emotion invested. It felt against all the good game tactics and strategies that I had ever known. It felt completely against what I considered to be sound match play, particularly against this type of an opponent.

Then it happened, just as we had predicted, I got hit in the face with the racket. My cheek was bleeding, and I had to stop the blood before we could continue. Even this did not bring me to my senses to change my game. I simply said to myself, "I always knew I was going to be hit." However, it did remind me that we were getting close to the end of the match, and things were starting to get desperate. Something needed to change; and if it was not going to be my opponent losing, it had better be me winning. Again, as my coach mopped the blood off my face, she said, "You must play the ball short."

Back on the court nothing changed, I was still hitting firmly to the back of the court and losing. Finally, with two points left in the match, I figured, "What the heck," I will hit a short ball and see what happens. I was sure my opponent thought she had the match in the bag and was picturing herself holding the trophy. She probably was even writing her acceptance speech in her head. Whatever was going on with her end of things, when I hit the drop, she didn't react. I mean she was like a deer in headlights. She did not move for the ball. Shocking as it was to me, I said, "My goodness, my coach was right! Let's try that again!" I went for a short ball the first chance I had – the same result. My opponent looked as though she had on lead shoes.

Wow! This was exciting! Could I actually turn the game around if I let go of what I believed I should do and started to do what was effective? I kept hitting short balls to eventually win that game and save myself from an embarrassing defeat – at least I had not been beaten 3 games to zero! Gratefully I got off the court at the end of the game and again my coach said, "Keep hitting your shots short." I could not believe it would continue to work. Surely my opponent would know that I was going to now hit every ball I could short, and she for sure would anticipate this to take away my effectiveness. No, that did not happen, and I became bolder and more audacious reaping great reward and the fourth game. Now we were tied two games each.

The last game was the decider and the winner took the title. The Vancouver crowd was now on my side. I had made Canada my home 7 years earlier and even represented Canada in Women's World Team events; and although my hometown was Toronto, I considered myself Canadian. I was finally giving these Canucks something to cheer for. It was over quickly with short shots being played by me from every part of the court. To play like this was unheard of, according to my beliefs. It was tactical suicide, but my coach was correct and it worked. Never once did my opponent adjust to this new game. Mind you, it was a huge, never to be forgotten lesson for me. I now know just how limiting and rigid our beliefs can be and just how hard it is to step out of them and change. However, change is our survival -both on and off the court.

How does this relate to your life, success, and general well-being?

This is what I have learnt over the years with great guidance from outstanding mentors who have continually demonstrated more concern for my well-being than I have shown myself. So often in life, we do not venture forth for fear of failure, being rejected, judged, laughed at or scorned. All of these notions are simply beliefs to which we can either attach importance or not. It is, however, far too easy to use a non-supportive belief to be a reason or excuse for non-action. We have all heard stories of great successes, but rarely do these people speak of the thousands of failures that lead to their success. They do not mention the humiliations, the disappointments and the learning that happened on the way. Most people pretend they were either born with incredible talent or they could always hit a ball, sell real estate, make money online, or speak comfortably in front of thousands.

Now that we know there will be a learning curve on anything we do and that we have two choices, to either grow or shrink, recognizing our beliefs may be uncomfortable, but that will not let stop our growth. My solution is to treat everything I do now as a practice. If it is practice, in my logic, I am not expecting myself to be brilliant because I am practicing and, therefore, still in the learning stage. I simply look for small improvements. I look for little wins, little corrections and small advancements. I am not looking for perfection. Even sloppy success will be great for me for now; and as I get more reps under my belt, I will expect my success to be slightly less sloppy.

People love to criticize and correct. Well, I can be happy in the knowledge that they can go crazy with me! I am going to give them plenty of opportunity to criticize and correct. I am, however, going to be growing and changing in the process with my knowledge and skills increasing.

In addition to sloppy success and handling criticism, we also have to learn to trust our senses. In this match, that taught me so much, there were three levels of trust that I experienced. First, I had to trust the advice I was being given. Believe me, clearly I was not, until I had my back against the wall and was staring defeat in the face, desperate enough to try something I thought to be radical.

This was the first lesson. If you go to someone who knows more and has more experience and insight and you have asked for help and advice, it might be smart to listen to them and not to your own limiting, often cautious and protective beliefs. Beliefs are fickle and capricious and can turn on a dime whenever convenient in your mind. It is easy to find excuses not to do something or reasons why you did. Be humble, listen to suggestions and execute actions to the very best of your ability. That is the only fair thing to do when you have sought advice and it has been proffered.

The second lesson: Once someone has genuinely given advice to you and you have implemented it, look for the result with your senses. Trust what your senses are telling you, particularly your eyes. Think about it, most people to whom you go for advice and help, actually want you to succeed. They are probably telling you what they would do in the same situation, and they are trying to give you good advice. Let's face it; it does no one's reputation any good to be associated with a supposed failure. That being said, look for how the advice can help you. Where will it take you? Give it a fair shot. Once you see positive results keep doing it, because just like any match, you never change a winning game.

Lesson number three: Once on the path to success, remember how you got there and who really helped. This must translate into gratitude and humility. You implemented the strategy absolutely, but others helped you become and grow and there needs to be acknowledgement in order to learn and grow some more. Should you make implementation all you do, you will become very limited in taking advice and counsel from others – as you already know it all! In my opinion, this is definitely not a great way to go through life.

Know where you want to go, hold that vision like a destination in your mind's eye, and walk daily towards it, one step at a time. Note the word walk. Few of us run to where we want to go and rarely do we get there directly and quickly (although your beliefs will always tell you nothing is ever quick enough).

Enjoy the journey, as THIS moment is never coming back. But your beliefs could!

ABOUT BARB

Barb Cooper is a best-selling author and world-class coaching expert who is regularly sought to help at provincial, national and international levels, coaching all aspects of performance, both in sport and business.

Based now in Toronto Canada, Barb Cooper has been involved in squash for the past 35 years. Provincially and internationally she has represented Great Britain, England and Canada. Being in the top 10 in the world and owning 10 world masters squash titles, makes her a unique coach, able to create great change by identifying strengths and weaknesses in any team or organization. She draws on her experience as a Master Learning Facilitator, which gives her skills in managing conflict, psychology of performance, coaching and leading effectively and making ethical decisions. As a past Director of Operations for one of the largest fitness clubs in Canada and as Director of Squash, Cooper is consulted on aspects of team building, mindset and general operations.

Cooper is the proud recipient of the Syl Apps Ontario Sport Award and the National Achievement Award for the province of Ontario, and she is the only Level 5 Squash Coach in Canada.

To learn more about Barb Cooper visit http://www.commited2life.acnibo.com or http://www.helpmysquashgame.com , or call 1-416-892-0583

CHAPTER 7

PRICELESS SMILES

BY EMILY LETRAN

It was a Wednesday afternoon in the winter, several years ago. The clouds were grey and gloomy, scattered with ominous shapes. The sky was ash black, looking almost fragile, like it was about to fall. That day might have been the saddest day ever in sunny Southern California.

My assistant Martha knocked on my office door, "You have a patient in room 2 for a check up." I walked over and in the dental chair was a lady wearing sunglasses. She wore a grey jacket and blue jeans; and her head was a little down, so I could not see the expression on her face. "Hi, Mrs. O'Neil," I said, glancing at the name on the chart, "How's it going?" As soon as I finished the sentence, my gut feeling told me

I should not have asked. Mrs. O'Neil looked up without removing her sunglasses. Her lips trembled, "It's not good... my husband, Joe, just died." I was speechless!

 My patients shared stories with me all the time, but I felt there was something different about THIS story. Mrs. O'Neil slowly told me that her husband was in an accident at work, where some heavy equipment fell and killed him. That happened Monday. As of today, Wednesday, she still could not see his body because "OSHA was still investigating the accident." I let her finished her story then I asked the unavoidable, stupid question. "Shouldn't you be... doing things to take care of his funeral instead of being here...what can I do for you?"

The sunglasses came off Mrs. O'Neil's face. I could feel the tears coming up in my own eyes as I heard her answer... "You see, Dr. Letran, I am here to get my teeth. I lost my upper denture. Just last week Joe gave me money to get my new teeth. He said he wanted to see my beautiful smile again. Now he's gone, but I want to get the teeth...for him."

There was not a dry eye in the office. I was crying, the assistants were crying and the patient was crying. In our profession, we know the smiles are priceless, because that's part of who we are, how we show our beauty, confidence, personality, and how the world sees us. Mrs. O'Neil, in this case, just missed the opportunity to show the man she loved her beautiful smile once again.

I started the exam for Mrs. O'Neil and recommended a complete upper denture and a lower partial denture because she only had her lower front teeth. Since her lips had fallen in without the cheek support offered by natural teeth and jawbone, she looked at least six to seven years older than her true age. We needed to make the dentures fast because, hopefully, the funeral would happen in about a week – as soon as she would get her husband's body back. I told her I would try my absolute best and got on the phone with my lab technician Bill.

There were four steps in making the dentures. I told Bill he would have one day in between each visit to make it perfect, rather than three to four working days, as in a regular case. I was bossy, and luckily he was listening. We proceeded to take the molds for the dentures, making sure that we captured all the details of her mouth to ensure proper fit of the dentures. Martha carefully poured up the model in yellow stone and told the lab to come pick up in one hour.

During her second visit, we took the measurement of Mrs. O'Neil's bite. To determine how tall and wide her teeth should be I asked Mrs. O'Neil to go through certain sounds where her lips had to come together and her "teeth" almost touched. I asked her to smile and marked the midline where the two front teeth would line up with the nose. I went through every step I would normally do with a denture patient to ensure I could make the most natural, beautiful and good fitting dentures. In her case, time was a factor. Any mistake would set us back painfully!

Mrs. O'Neil then chose the color of her new teeth for the dentures. She picked the one that matched her remaining lower natural teeth and cried again while looking in the mirror. She shared with us that she was going through her husband's "things" and missed him more. There was not much we could say to share her grief. We all sat, listened and reflected on how fleeting life can be – how a short and unexpected moment can leave the first, or in this case, the last, memory of someone we love.

The third appointment came, and I was extremely nervous. If the teeth looked good, we would be fine. If they didn't look right, we would be set back another appointment to re-set the teeth, and that meant TWO days. I was worried that I would let my patient down. I was worried that she would let her husband down...on his funeral day...without seeing her beautiful smile. I was so uptight that I did not notice my whole staff was also worrying!

Mrs. O'Neil arrived and sat in the chair, looking nervous... just like I was! I gave her the dentures. The fit was perfect. The teeth looked nice because she had picked a good color to match the tone of her skin and the rest of her natural teeth. "Please smile for me," I asked. The forced smile was de-cent, with all the teeth and the pink gum in harmony with the curves of her lips. She tapped her teeth together to check the bite. "How do you like the freezing weather?" I asked, and as she answered, I listened carefully to see how natural and accurate the words were pronounced with the new teeth.

Lastly, I handed her the big hand mirror. "I'd like for you to take a look," I said, and slowly walked out of the room. I always do that to let the patient look at the teeth themselves, on their own, without feeling that they need to approve the work while I'm standing there.

I was hardly three steps away when she burst into loud sobbing, "Oh my God!" she said, choking with tears. "Joe would have loved these!" My feet were glued to the ground. Mrs. O'Neil continued sobbing until the whole office was in tears again. "Do you like the way they look?" I spoke gently.

"Yes, Dr. Letran, they look beautiful!" She smiled through her tears. It was the first genuine smile I had seen on her face during the last few appointments. "If you like them the way they are, I will ask the lab to finish them by the day after to-morrow." "Yes! I'm ready for Joe's funeral now!" Her face was beaming with joy. She left the office and could not wait to come back.

On the day of the denture delivery, our office was happy be-cause we completed our mission – the mission of helping our patient gain back her confidence, improve her image and be at peace with her husband. Mrs. O'Neil put the final dentures on. The dentures helped her cheeks perk up and smoothed out the aging lines. Her new teeth made her look more youth-ful because there were no more drooping lips. She actually showed us her smile, a priceless smile, not a forced one. And there were more tears, but tears of happiness!

She went around the office, hugging everyone. We wished her peace and sent our prayers with her. Mrs. O'Neil left the office a different woman than when she first came in 8 days before.

I felt I had done my very small part to make her day of "saying goodbye" to her husband much more special. I was thankful I had the knowledge to do my job and support from the team of lab and assistants helping me through the whole process. I realized my profession was more than working on the teeth. It was the creation and preservation of that price-less connection, the smiles between human beings, in their family lives, on a daily basis or for a special occasion.

A few weeks later, during a busy afternoon, my assistant Martha ran in and told me, "You've got to come outside. Someone is here to see you."

In the lobby was a beautiful young lady with a huge poinsettia at least 4 feet tall. She smiled.

"You don't know me, Dr. Letran, but I'm here for my mom. I wanted to bring you these." She handed me the flowers, a note card, and gave me a big hug. "My mom took a trip out of town after the funeral. She sent her love. And our family is thankful too."

The young lady left, and I opened the note card. It said her dad must be happy looking down from heaven. I felt so blessed because I was able to make a difference in Mrs. O'Neil's and her family's life.

So, you may ask, what is a priceless smile in life? My answer, it is the smile of the baby when the first two lower front teeth come in, and the young mother sees them as little pearls. It is the smile on the face of a little girl who just got asked to her first school dance. It may be the smiles of the high school team after winning a championship game. Certainly, you can relate to the smiles of the groom and bride on their special wedding day. Then there are the smiles of anniversaries, reunions, family get-togethers, birthdays, showers and graduations. We communicate with smiles, share our thoughts and feelings with smiles, and sometimes we don't realize the impact a smile can make, how priceless a smile can be, as was the case of Mrs. O'Neil, when it was a little too late. Time is indifferent; it keeps on moving, changing people and changing things. What we have to hold on to is the memories made with those lasting smiles.

As a dentist, it is my job to serve my patients and help them keep their beautiful, priceless smiles. I advise parents to bring in young children as early as age two to have their first check up exam. I follow the teeth development and may recommend braces when there are signs of crowding or poor jaw relationship. In the adults, I deal with cases of teeth chipping, needing porcelain veneers; teeth turning yellow that benefit from a Zoom! Whitening session; teeth overlapping that require Invisalign to correct and preserve the health of the gum; or teeth worn down from grinding and aging, where a full mouth rehabilitation is necessary to restore proper bite.

With our seniors staying healthy and enjoying a full social life, I have made numerous natural-looking dentures where the artificial "gum" is almost clear, showing through the true color of the patient's soft tissue. Nowadays, implants can replace missing teeth, and the patient can smile and chew just like they have teeth of their own. We also use implants to support and tighten dentures when the patients have most or all of their teeth missing. The implants preserve the bone in the jaw, thus helping the patient keep beautiful facial profile.

Modern dentistry has the means to help develop and preserve priceless smiles. Dental health should not be about pain and cost. It should be part of a life-long investment, just as annual physical exams, and hopefully – not to be a "late" part in a chapter of a relationship.

We don't know whose life we touch on a daily basis. Think of a business and its customers, a doctor and his patients, a teacher and his or her students, a pastor and his or her church members. The smiles are our priceless "assets" that are uniquely ours, and others deserve our smiles, attention, and care.

Our dental health is related to our systemic health; we can detect certain conditions such as diabetes or oral cancer just from a routine dental exam, aided by other devices, such as the Velscope used for oral cancer screening.

The dentist, as part of the health professional team, should be updated and consulted about your general health condition. We want to lead healthy, successful lives, and our priceless smiles are certainly a big part of that. I cannot tell you how many times someone commented to me that they got through a job interview with the confidence that the new smiles had given them, or a bride-to-be, getting ready for the big day, become ecstatic with a whitening make-over, and yes, the 70 + gentleman who started dating again after his implant-supported dentures are made, tight and good-as-new.

I am thankful every day that I can make a small difference in people's lives by preserving and enhancing their price-less smiles. The family dentist is a health team member who wants to help you take care of one of your greatest assets, the priceless smile that reflects confidence and wonderful self-image – improving and changing your life for the better.

And, as a business owner, every day as I am bombarded with challenging situations, like a delivery order that does not come, a patient that shows up late, or a case that does not fin-ish as expected, I am there, out front, giving it my all. Through the stressful times, I remind myself that business is just a part of the human relationship, and it is that relationship that we strive to make perfect every day, whether with a trustful hand-shake, an intimate hug, or a happy, priceless smile, to make life more meaningful and enjoyable for all of us.

ABOUT EMILY

Dr. Emily Letran is a general dentist who owns three multi-specialty group practices in Southern California. She received her Bachelor of Science in Biology from UC Riverside (*magna cum laude*, Phi Beta Kappa). She is a graduate of UCLA School of Dentistry (Dean's Apollonian Scholarship) and received her Master of Science in Oral Biology from UCLA at the same time. After graduation she participated in the General Practice Residency at Loma Linda VA Medical Center in Loma Linda, CA. and a mini-residency at Rancho Los Amigos Medical Center in Downey, CA., where she attained additional training in treating geriatric and medically compromised patients.

As a mother of three, Dr. Letran creatively balances work, family life, after-school life and her personal life as a growing entrepreneur. She continuously takes courses in clinical dentistry, practice management and marketing, striving to improve her skills to better serve patients. Her favorite activities include reading, writing, and "hanging out" with her three children – whether playing tennis, watching Netflix or window-shopping at the mall.

For Dr. Letran, it is an honor and privilege to be part of her patients' lives. As she watches kids growing up, grandparents getting old, the passing of spouses, the courage of the people left behind, individuals going through tough times like job loss or marital separation, she is reminded that the most important thing in life are the relationships we build with other human beings. She is proud to be a small part of these relationships – the ones she shares with patients.

Dr. Letran is actively involved in professional organizations, because she knows peers are an invaluable source of new information, and membership in these organizations lets her gain insight into events that are shaping the future of dentistry. She also engages in community service, sponsoring multiple local school and charity events, including the Annual Free Dentistry Day in local communities, where she and her dental team work for two days to provide free dentistry for the less fortunate in area communities.

For additional information on how to create and preserve "priceless smiles," please contact Dr. Letran at:

Foothill Dental Center
837 W. Foothill Blvd., Monrovia, CA., 91016
(626) 305-5722
www.cosmeticdentistmonrovia.com

Mountain View Dental Group
4639 N. Peck Rd., El Monte, CA. 91732
(626) 444-9281,
www.myelmontedentist.com

Universal Family Dental Practice
10012 Garvey Avenue, Suite #11, El Monte, CA. 91733
(626) 433-1300
www.myelmontedentist.com

CHAPTER 8

A BEAUTIFUL SMILE:

A KEY TO A BRIGHT AND SUCCESSFUL FUTURE

BY WILLIAM CALDON, DMD

The young man that sat in my dental chair was covered with tattoos and body piercings. He came to us from his workplace, because a wrench that he had been using had slipped and snapped off his front tooth. After I had examined him and told him we could help him, I left the room to await the taking of the X-Ray. The patient embarrassedly looked around and then quietly asked my wife, who happened to be my dental assistant that day, if the doctor really could make his tooth look natural again. My wife told him, "Of course, why do you ask?" He replied, "Well, I was just wondering, because I'm really self-conscious about the way that I look." When my wife told me the story, we both had a good laugh at the irony. We both realized that even this young man, who flaunted conventional decorum with his ubiquitous body art and abundant impaling jewelry, had a nascent understanding of the importance of an attractive smile.

Another patient, a middle-aged man, who worked as a custodian in a high school about 80 miles away, came to us with no upper teeth. He had a huge gag reflex and was unable to wear traditional dentures. He stated that he was able to eat without problems, but because of his lack of teeth, he had been too embarrassed to smile for years. He told us that all he wanted was some upper front teeth so that he could smile without shame. His mother took out a second mortgage on her home so that he could afford dental implants. When we inserted the implant restorations and let him see himself in the mirror, this tough, burley he-man shed crocodile tears of joy. He beamed as he told us that this was the first time he had been able to smile for as long as he could remember.

Although both of these gentlemen were blue-collar workers and were not likely to become Fortune 500 CEOs, both realized the importance of an attractive smile in today's society. And these are not isolated incidents. We see these life changing occurrences almost every day in our practice. A radiant smile is universally recognized as a sign of health, vitality and success. When we look at models and spokespersons in national magazines and on television, they universally display lustrous smiles. The Hollywood stars that we see on the big screen, with the exception of Steve Buscemi and a few character actors, all seem to have that perfect smile.

So, it's obvious that a beautiful smile is universally recognized as a sign of beauty in today's society. But as I mentioned earlier, an attractive smile is also identified as a sign of health and vitality. It is no accident that we have this impression. Infections in the mouth, in addition to having an unappealing appearance, have been linked to several serious systemic diseases such as heart disease, diabetes and pre-term, low birth weight babies. Also, mouth infections, if left untreated can be life threatening. In addition, oral infections are frequently the cause of halitosis or bad breath.

Fortunately, there are a myriad of dental procedures available today to painlessly improve smiles and enhance health. Some of the least expensive and least invasive measures to protect and maintain an already attractive smile are preventive in nature. Let's discuss some of those treatments.

With the introduction of fluoride into many of our water systems, tooth decay or *Dental Caries* is less prevalent than what was seen several years ago. However, it is still a disease that affects as much as 94% of the population. Dental caries is an infection of the teeth mediated by bacteria that metabolize the carbohydrates (sugars and starches) that we consume to produce an acid, which destroys the teeth. There are several approaches available that can help prevent the onset of tooth decay or dental caries:

1. Mechanically removing the bacteria with efficient daily brushing and flossing can effectively reduce the amount of decay producing bacteria. Many of the toothpastes available today have the added benefits of carrying fluoride, whitening materials and remineralizing agents to the teeth.

2. Although there is no silver bullet that will selectively eliminate all the bad bacteria, there are rinses available that can reduce the number of pathologic bacteria.

3. The production of the acid by the bacteria can be minimized by reducing the amount of refined sugars and starches that they are exposed to by consuming less of those types of food.

4. Exposure to the proper amount of fluoride as the tooth is developing, as well as, after the tooth has erupted can make the tooth's enamel more resistant to the effects of the acid that the bacteria produce or that we consume in sodas and other products.

5. Plastic sealants can be flowed into the grooves on the biting surfaces of back teeth that are not well cleansed by the toothbrush bristles and consequently harbor decay producing bacteria.

However, once the decay process begins, we have at our disposal a wide array of treatments available to restore the health of the tooth depending on the extent of the disease.

If the decay is deep and has reached the nerve of the tooth, often the tooth can be saved with root canal therapy. Although root canal treatments have a bad reputation in common culture, they usually can be accomplished painlessly in one appointment and add years of service to the tooth.

If the decay is extensive, but has not reached the nerve of the tooth or a root canal has been successfully completed, the tooth can be restored with onlays or crowns. These can be fabricated from very strong, esthetic, metal-free ceramics, sometimes in one appointment with Computerized Assisted

Design (CAD) techniques.

If the decay is less extensive, the tooth can be restored with a cosmetic composite resin material that is available in a myriad of shades and opacities and can be bonded and made to blend in seamlessly to the remaining tooth structure.

Dental caries though is not the only common infection of the mouth that can have an effect on the cosmetics of a smile or the acceptability of one's breath. *Periodontal Disease,* a bacterial infection that leads to destruction of the gum tissue and supporting bone, can cause more of the tooth to be exposed (becoming "long in the tooth") and lead to sensitivity, mobility and sometimes the eventual loss of the tooth.

Fortunately, some of the same methods that are effective in preventing tooth decay are also effective in preventing the beginning and advance of periodontal disease. Efficient daily brushing and flossing, antibacterial rinses and frequent dental cleanings can disrupt the bacterial colonies that cause the destruction of the supporting structures of the teeth. Unfortunately, periodontal disease is for the most part a silent, painless malady that is often not evident until it's too late for the tooth to be saved. So frequent dental visits and early interventions are the keys to managing periodontal disease. Also there are several newer less invasive ways to treat periodontal disease without the painful side effects of the surgical techniques that have been used in the past. The FDA has approved a laser protocol that encourages the reattachment of tissue back to the surface of the tooth as opposed to the surgical procedures that caused the exposure of more of the tooth's root surface leading to sensitivity and the "long in the tooth" appearance.

Although infectious diseases of the mouth can cause our smiles to be less than ideal, other factors like genetic make-up can be responsible for an unattractive smile, or sometimes it's merely years of drinking wine, coffee and tea that can lead to stained and discolored teeth.

The newer, stronger, more esthetic materials available today provide us with a wide array of treatment modalities for smile enhancement depending on the situation. Common treatments are among the following:

1. Whitening or bleaching of the teeth can be accomplished with the use of peroxide impregnated strips bought over the counter or more effectively by applying the bleaching material using custom fitted trays supplied by the dentist. For more immediate needs, such as an impending wedding or family photo, whitening can often be accomplished at one appointment in the dentist's office.

2. In some situations, simply performing a cosmetic re-contouring (a gentle reshaping of the teeth by removing a slight bit of enamel) combined with whitening procedures may be all that is necessary to achieve a radiant smile.

3. Ceramic veneers are also available to enhance the smile. These are thin porcelain restorations placed over the outside of the tooth that can improve the shape and color of the tooth. Some newer materials are so thin and so strong that zero to minimal preparation of the tooth is necessary.

4. Porcelain crowns (caps) are an option too. In some cases, it is necessary to remove more of the tooth

to achieve the desired end, resulting in a ceramic restoration that covers the entire tooth. With today's materials, this can be achieved with extraordinarily life-like results without the "Chiclet" smiles that we used to see with the older ceramics.

5. Composite resins are often referred to as "bonding." These are the same materials used to restore decayed teeth. Resins can be effectively bonded to the teeth and can be used to close spaces between the teeth or reshape the tooth into a more ideal appearance.

6. Dental implants are another method used in today's dentistry. Implants are achieved using titanium posts integrated directly into the jawbone. They are a predictable, effective way to replace missing teeth with extremely esthetic results.

7. In the case where it is impractical or unaffordable to replace missing teeth with implants or bridges, the use of cosmetic acrylics or porcelains, flexible materials and strong light weight metals, alone or in combination in removable appliances, can often be used to achieve spectacular results.

8. Orthodontics today can be used with people of almost any age as a single modality or in combination with most of the above-mentioned treatments. And the orthodontics of today doesn't always have to use the "braces" that we, and our parents, knew growing up. Often times, tooth colored brackets, bands, wires and elastics can be used. Sometimes the brackets can be placed on the backside of the teeth. In some cases, clear plastic trays that are almost completely invisible can be used

to move the teeth into the desired position.

Becky (not her real name) is an attractive, outgoing middle-aged woman who works in our office. She has a great sense of humor and likes to smile, however, whenever she returns out west to visit family, her older sister drags out Becky's old nickname of "Bucky" and reminds her of her protruding upper front teeth and exaggerated overbite. Needless to say, Becky doesn't like to go home and be constantly bludgeoned by her sister with the reminder of her less than perfect smile. Becky has opted to undergo a short course of orthodontics to improve the appearance of her smile. She is doing it with her daughter, who is also undergoing orthodontics, so they can be supportive of one another as they move through the treatment. As the treatment progresses, Becky smiles more and gets more and more excited as she looks forward to the day when she can return for a visit and show her sister that she is no longer "Bucky" and can be treated with the respect she so deserves.

Laura (also not her real name) is a beautiful young woman who is scheduled to be married in several months. Both her upper and lower teeth have been severely crowded with several teeth twisted and overlapped. Laura also opted for a minor course of orthodontics with the removal of one of her lower front teeth and some bonding with esthetic composite resin material to close up the small residual spaces left by extraction. It is amazing to watch the transformation and to see Laura's and her family's excitements grow as her smile goes through its metamorphosis into a true thing of beauty. Laura's new, radiant smile surely will give her so much more joy and confidence on her wedding day.

Whether it is fair or not, we are often judged by other people on our appearance. How we are perceived and consequently treated by others can be critical to our self-esteem and can even be instrumental in seeking jobs or advancing within an organization. Our smile can be a critical part of this perception. Fortunately, we have at our disposal a wide array of measures to improve and preserve our smile. Some of these are preventive in nature and are relatively inexpensive and others are more involved and somewhat costly. However, all can be accomplished with minimal to no discomfort.

With the myriad of treatment modalities available, almost anyone can find an affordable treatment that will enhance the beauty of their smile and start them on the road to a more successful and brighter future.

ABOUT BILL

Dr. Bill Caldon was born in Covington Kentucky and is now a dentist practicing with his partners Dr. Mike O'Connor and Dr. D.J. O'Neill in upstate New York at the edge of the Adirondack Mountains and on the shores of beautiful Lake Champlain. He has a Bachelor's degree in Biology from Thomas More College in northern Kentucky and a Doctor of Dental Medicine (DMD) degree from the University of Louisville.

Dr. Caldon spent twenty years in the United States Air Force retiring as a Colonel. In 1985 he successfully completed an Air Force two-year Advanced Education Program in General Dentistry. During his Air Force career, Dr. Caldon taught courses in restorative dentistry, oral pathology, temporomandibular disorders, pediatric dentistry and orthodontics. He served as Director of a one-year Advanced Education Program in General Dentistry and commanded Dental Squadrons in England, New York and New Jersey, often serving as interim Hospital Commander. For three years he served as an Examiner on the Federal Services Board of General Dentistry.

Dr. Caldon is a fellow in the Academy of General Dentistry, a Diplomate of the American Board of General Dentistry and is a member of the American Dental Association, International College of Dentist, American Dental Implant Association, New York State Dental Association and New York's Fourth District Dental Society. He routinely attends well over 100 hours of continuing education per year and is certified in Oral Conscious Sedation and Short Term Orthodontics.

Dr. Caldon has been married to Margaret, his childhood sweetheart, for 38 years and has four fantastic children and, at last count, five beautiful grandchildren. Visit Dr. Caldon's website at www.HighPeaksDental.com or contact him at WilliamCaldon@yahoo.com

CHAPTER 9

EIGHT THINGS YOU CAN DO TODAY TO INCREASE YOUR HEALTH AND LONGEVITY

BY KAZI ANAM M.S.,R.PH.,C.Ht.

John glances at his watch – only nine minutes until he needs to be back at his desk, organize and present his project to the group. He finishes the last bite of his half-pound hamburger and decides to gulp down a bit more of his soda before dashing out the door of the diner.

Just the thought of his project sends a new rush of adrenaline coursing through his body as he reaches the elevator in his office building. Deciding to forgo the wait for the elevator, lest he lose valuable seconds of work before his presentation, John takes the stairs two at a time. When he reaches his desk on the 3ʳᵈ floor, he glances again at his watch and realizes it's time to go, so he grabs his laptop and heads for the meeting room. His chest is pounding. Would they accept his ideas?

Post-presentation, John is largely relieved that it's gone extremely well. His relief is short-lived, however. As he reaches his desk, John feels a tightness squeezing at his chest, coupled with pain almost like heartburn. He drops into his leather desk chair and figures the hamburger did not digest properly. By now the pain has subsided a bit, so John begins to flip through his planner and to-do list for the remainder of the day. Before he can finish his review of the planner, he feels an intense pain in his chest and shortness of breath coupled with dizziness. He reaches for the phone. John's whole life starts to play in agonizing slow motion through his mind. Is he having a heart attack? Is he going to die? John just celebrated his 43ʳᵈ birthday the previous week. Then his thoughts and consciousness slip away.

In his sleep, John hears unrecognized voices. He doesn't feel like opening his eyes yet. He wants to turn over in bed, but something is restraining him. Slowly, he opens his eyes to an unfamiliar world. "Where am I?" John mutters. "Honey, you're going to be okay," replies his wife, Emily.

John tries to sit up, but Emily keeps him down and softly murmurs, "The doctor said you're out of danger now." Finally, reality creeps back into John's brain. He's had a heart attack, and he's in the hospital now. "Why?"

John visited his doctor annually for a routine physical. Everything seemed to be okay. He knew he was a bit overweight -- he grabbed fast food frequently because of the hectic pace of his job--he smoked a pack of cigarettes daily, and he never managed his stress. But John blamed his doctor, his workload and anything he could think of, except himself.

John is not alone.

In the United States there are over 1 million heart attacks every year. Many of these heart attacks could have been prevented by being proactive not reactive. Placing blame on someone else does not help. Everyone needs to be in charge of his own health.

So, how long can a person live?

After much research, I am of the opinion that it is quite possible for a person to live up to 120 years. Barring an accident, one of the following preventable diseases will most likely cause your death:

Cardiovascular diseases (heart attack, stroke etc)

Cancer
Diabetes
Alzheimer's disease
Infections
Kidney related diseases
Liver related diseases
Medication Side effects

I know what you are probably thinking right now. My dad has this disease, my grandpa had this one; I am genetically likely to get it too. Stop right there!

I want to inspire you to celebrate life and take charge of your health so that you can stay healthier longer and live to your fullest potential. You literally have the fountain of youth at your disposal. Drink from it! You know your potential causes of death and, except for an accident, you can follow my guidelines and increase your longevity. Instead of focusing on the things we cannot alter, like genetics, let's concentrate on eight things you can do to improve your health and longevity today.

1. Heredity and lifestyle are the most important risk factors. You cannot do much about your heredity, but you can manipulate all the others in the above list to minimize your risk.

Let's take a look at lifestyle. What type of lifestyle do you lead? Is it balanced or unbalanced? Do you eat well? Do you sleep well? Do you smoke? Do you exercise?

You most likely already know smoking is not good for you. Did you know that smoking not only affects the lungs; it also affects the whole body? When you smoke, billions of toxic particles enter your body including carbon monoxide and nicotine. All these have very significant health consequences. If you are a smoker, your goal should be to quit smoking – today. There are many methods available to help you to stop smoking. My research shows that hypnosis is a very effective way to quit smoking. Instead of trying to quit smoking by yourself, consider seeking professional help for this.

Do you exercise? Be honest. If you don't, start immediately. Choose an exercise you think you will enjoy and can fit into your lifestyle. You need to find out what form of exercise that you enjoy, so sample some different things. If you don't enjoy the type of exercise you are doing, you will not do it routinely or you will stop doing it altogether. I am often asked, "What is the best type of exercise?" My answer always is "the type that you are going to enjoy." Whether you like jogging, walking, bicycling, swimming, dancing, zumba or yoga, it does not matter. All of these are aerobic exercises. Additionally, you need to do some resistance exercise or exercise with weights. Resistance exercise strengthens and builds muscle, which helps your body burn calories more efficiently.

2. Your body weight should be close to your ideal body weight. You need to pay a lot of attention here. Almost 70% of the US population is somewhat overweight. Being overweight increases the risk of developing any of the diseases listed above. After lots of research and working with many individuals who want to lose weight, I came to the conclusion that you need to address following issues to maintain optimum weight.

Check functionality of your thyroid gland. Sometimes blood tests do not accurately reflect the status of your thyroid function. You can check this by measuring your body temperature as soon as you wake up. Use an oral thermometer to check your oral temperature as soon as you awaken but before getting out of the bed. Your average

temperature should be 98F. If your temperature is consistently below 98F, you should consult with a health care provider to help you to boost your thyroid function.

Check cortisol level (Stress hormone)
Check your Insulin sensitivity
Check other hormones balance

Review the adverse side effects of any medications you are taking. Some medications have a tendency to increase weight. For example: Corticosteroids, certain blood pressure medications, insulin, as well as some medication for depression can cause weight gain.

Take notice if you start to gain weight after introducing a particular medication. If this happens, consult with your physician and pharmacist. In many cases there might be a suitable alternative.

Increase your basal metabolic rate, that is, your energy expenditure while at rest.

Finally, *add supplements* to reduce absorption of carbohydrates and control sugar spikes following a meal, as well as, to increase the basal metabolic rate. And remember that exercise can assist you with weight loss. For weight loss, concentrated, quick bursts of intense exercise are more beneficial than prolonged, steady exercise like the treadmill.

Weight loss is a complex issue. It is not impossible to lose few pounds following a diet, but the hardest part is to keep it off permanently. I recommend that anyone, who wants permanent weight loss, should consult with a healthcare provider who specializes in weight loss.

3. Good dietary habits will affect your health and longevity. In my consultations, I find that a majority of my clients do not begin their day with a good breakfast. Do you skip breakfast because you are in a hurry to get out the door or because you believe you are saving calories? If this is you, I recommend you start your day with a solid breakfast that includes a portion of fruit, protein, good fat and a small portion of a complex carbohydrate such as quinoa, barley or oatmeal. Avoid bread, cereal, pasta, rice, wheat etc.

Your main meal of the day should be breakfast. In the morning, your digestive system works most efficiently, and a good breakfast will keep you energetic throughout the day. Your last meal of the day should be light and consist of protein, vegetables and good fat like olive oil with no sugary dessert or fruit. At night your digestion slows down considerably, thus a heavy dinner will not digest properly and may cause weight gain. Snacks between meals should consist of some type of raw nuts such as almonds, cashews, pistachios or walnuts.

4. Sleep is the next major component to your optimal health. An average adult requires about 7-8 hours per day. During sleep your body does all the restoration and repair work you need as well as secretes different hormones that are essential to good health. Keep your room dark while sleeping, as darkness is important for melatonin secretion. Melatonin is a hormone secreted in the brain that regulates circadian rhythm. If you have difficulty falling asleep, try to stop eating 2-3 hours before sleep time. Stop watching TV or working on a computer about one hour before your bedtime, instead read a book until you are sleepy. If these suggestions do not help, first try a supplement with tryptophan. If you still have a problem, you can add melatonin. Ultimately, if you are still having sleep troubles, seek the advice of a professional.

5. Manage Stress. During stress your body releases adrenaline and cortisol to help you face challenges. But too much of these substances are counter-productive. You need to devise a system to help your body slow down. You can reset your stress triggers through exercise, yoga, listening to music, laughing (watch a funny movie or show), walking, prayer or meditation. Did you notice that some of your healthy lifestyle choices would also help you to reduce stress?

6. Vitamins and supplements intake are a critical component of your health that your healthcare provider might not mention to you. Unfortunately, many healthcare providers are not fully aware of the benefits of vitamins and supplements. Why do you need supplementation even when you eat well? At this time, even with food in abundant supply for most people, our food supply does not have the nutritional value that it did 50 or 100 years ago. Our lifestyles are more indoors than outdoors, and we are exposed to a plethora of gadgets such as computers, cell phones and fluorescent lights that can zap nutritional stores.

Here is a test for you. Even if you eat a balanced meal and you happen to spend the bulk of your time indoors, ask your doctor to check your vitamin D level at your next visit. Ask that he check your 25-hydroxy Vitamin D level. This is the most accurate way to measure Vitamin D. A normal blood level should be between 30 to 74 nanograms per milliliter (ng/ml). In my personal opinion, the optimum hydroxy Vitamin D level should be between 55 and 70 ng/ml. I have looked at dozens of individuals' Vitamin D levels and did not find a single individual to have optimum levels prior to supplementation with Vitamin D3. Vitamin D3 is extremely important to immune health and research shows that this can prevent many types of cancer. Therefore, proper intake of vitamins and supplements is essential to maintaining optimal health. In my practice, I have noticed that most people have no clue what type of supplements they should be consuming. In my opinion, one needs to avoid the synthetic vitamins and supplements even though organic and natural supplements cost a bit more.

Before starting supplementation, consult with a healthcare practitioner who is experienced with vitamins and supplements. In my practice, I have developed four levels of supplements categories based on individual needs. Level 1 supplements could be used by almost anyone; they include a good multivitamin and mineral formula, a good B-complex formula, 1000 to 5000 units of vitamin D3 daily, 1000 to 4000 mg of vitamin C daily (preferably in powder form) and 2 to 4 grams of fish oil daily. To this we add Probiotics at least 2 servings daily (at least 5 billion microorganism per serving) to increase immune health and digestion.

7. Detoxification and Internal Cleansing. Sounds intense; it is, intensely important. It is extremely important to adopt a program of detoxification and internal cleansing. Let's face it; we live in a toxic world. Daily we are exposed to numerous toxins and chemicals with the potential to accumulate in our bodies and vital organs. Without detoxification these can cause weight gain, cancer, Alzheimer's, arthritis, multiple schlerosis and many other diseases. In my practice I recommend and use Dr. Natura detoxification products and have had wonderful experience with these detox and cleansing products.

8. Medication Management. How you manage your medication is extremely important for your health and longevity this includes both prescription *and* any over-the-counter medications you might be taking. First, remember that all medications have some sort adverse side effects. Approximately 100,000 persons die every year from adverse affects of medication.

Look in any household medicine cabinet and you will likely find a bottle of acetaminophen or the equivalent. Yet, most people in those same households don't realize that if used improperly acetaminophen can cause liver failure. In the United States, acetaminophen toxicity has replaced viral hepatitis as the most common cause of acute liver failure and is the second most common cause of liver failure requiring transplantation.

Another class of medications, called statins, reduces cholesterol but not without potential side effects. One side effect of statins is the depletion of Coenzyme Q10 in the body. Coenzyme Q10 has significant use in the heart for proper energy production. Anyone taking a statin drug should also supplement with coenzyme Q10.

Proper management of all medications begins with finding a pharmacist on whom you can rely. It could be a matter of life or death without the proper management. An excellent pharmacist will manage your medications, make note of possible interactions or contraindications, and he or she will consult with your physician to find a solution. Your pharmacist can help minimize side effects of your medications by recommending appropriate supplements and foods to optimize your health. Do not settle for just any pharmacist; choose the more competent one even if it means driving a bit further. Most people choose their hair stylist more carefully than they choose their pharmacist.

Do not wait until you, like John, wake up in a hospital bed before you make the changes that can help you live to 120 years old. Take charge of your health today!

ABOUT KAZI

KAZI ANAM M.S.,R.Ph.,C.Ht. is a pharmacist, health coach, certified hypnotist and the CEO of Dekalb Pharmacy and Wellness Center. Anam has been a practicing pharmacist for over 25 years; and as a pharmacist, he guides his clients to manage medications properly in order to achieve excellent outcomes with minimal adverse reactions.

As a health coach, Anam helps his clients to achieve good health and longevity using lifestyle modification, good nutrition and customized supplement selection. Currently, his main focus is assisting individuals with losing excess weight and keeping it off permanently. Besides individualized diet, exercise and supplement programs, Anam employs hypnosis to facilitate permanent weight loss for his clients. Kazi Anam was seen on ABC, CBS, NBC and Fox Affiliates.

CHAPTER 10

TO LIVE LONG AND PROSPER

BY SUNDARDAS D. ANNAMALAY

I was born with a cleft palate and cleft lip and started having surgical interventions beginning at six months of age. From then on, I had surgery every few years because of repeated infections. I was to spend the next 20 years having multiple surgeries and being on multiple courses of antibiotics yearly. I was also to spend most of the 20 years in mild to excruciating pain as a result of those interventions.

At six years of age, I was speech handicapped, hearing handicapped and brain damaged (maybe because of the birth trauma, infections and surgery). I was not to discover the extent and severity of the damage until I was in my late thirties. When I was 39, I had a brain scan and discovered, although

I was a right-brained person, the right side of my brain was damaged; so I had compensated by developing the left side of the brain especially the Wernicke's area. When I was attending a post-graduate training program on Autism at about age 44, I discovered I was autistic.

At 19 I had the last (or what I thought was my last) surgery. I decided that I was going to take control of my physical health. I started a regime of avoiding potential allergens that began to change my physiology and neurology. My allergies and frequent infections began to reduce, and my brain started "turning on." I began asking myself at 25, the following:

What is the secret of how we become ill on a cellular level?

How did our emotional state affect us on a cellular and molecular level?

I set out to answer the above questions. It was to take 15 years of undergraduate, graduate, postgraduate and postdoctoral study and research and almost two million dollars of personal investment before these questions were answered. When I came up with my tentative conclusions, I realized that it was actually the answer to: "What does it take for us to actualize our fullest potential from our cellular to our emotional levels?"

When I was about 38 my father died and my two best friends died. The sad part was that none of them needed to die when they did. While death is inevitable, I feel we should lead rich meaningful lives and die because our bodies are worn out and not because we did not how, or choose not to, take care of our bodies. They all died of modifiable risk factors for chronic disease. The leading risk factors globally for non-communicable diseases are raised blood pressure, tobacco use, raised blood sugar, physical inactivity, being overweight and obesity.

In prehistoric times, the physical changes in response to stress were an essential adaptation for meeting natural threats. Even in the modern world, the stress response can be an asset for raising levels of performance during critical events, such as a sports activity, an important meeting, or in situations of actual danger or crisis. If stress becomes persistent and low-level, however, all parts of the body's stress apparatus (the brain, heart, lungs, blood vessels, and muscles) become chronically over-activated or under-activated. Such chronic stress may produce physical or psychological damage over time.

By contrast, my paternal grandfather who died at just before 100 maintained a diet and lifestyle pattern that avoided all the above risk factors. He continued to be ambulant and lucid, giving after diner speeches in his nineties. My father by contrast started off with no illness, but by dint of 30 years of smoking, drinking and overworking developed hypertension, diabetes, heart disease and cancer in that order. Both my brother and I by the process of precise dietary modulation, exercise, nutrition and stress management are reaching our fiftieth year with only worn out knees and without the other markers of Syndrome X. So we know this is possible.

America is already on the verge of drowning in sick-care bankruptcy, but the situation is about to get even worse. According to a new study released by the *Organization for Economic Cooperation and Development*, three-fourths of Americans will be obese or overweight by 2020. That puts America in first place for the world competition to see which nation can create the most obese population.

According to the World Health Organization (WHO), non-communicable diseases (NCDs) are the leading cause of deaths worldwide. In 2008, of the 57 million deaths, 36 million people died due to NCDs. Deaths were attributed to cardiovascular diseases (48%), cancers (21%), chronic respiratory diseases (12%), and diabetes (3%).

New estimates from the World Health Organization indicate that chronic diseases place a grave economic burden on countries, and that this burden will increase if no action is taken to curb the epidemics. In 2005 the estimated losses in national income from heart disease, stroke and diabetes (reported in international dollars) were $18 billion in China, $11 billion in the Russian Federation, $9 billion in India and $3 billion dollars in Brazil.

In Malaysia the National Health Morbidity Survey data revealed that in adults, 20.7% were overweight and 5.8% obese (0.3% of whom had BMI values of >40.0 kg m (-2)); the prevalence of obesity was clearly greater in women than in men. In women obesity rates were higher in Indian and Malay women than in Chinese women, while in men, the Chinese recorded the highest obesity prevalence followed by the Malay and Indians.

Chronic disease prevention and control can no longer be ignored as an important means of poverty reduction, and more generally, economic development. Investment in chronic disease prevention programmes is essential for many low and middle income countries struggling to reduce poverty.

I studied with Dr Thomas Rau, MD of Paracelsus Klink,

Lustmühle, Switzerland who runs one of the premier German cancer clinics. Based on his research, I developed a cancer screening protocol after working with all the cancer patients who came to see me. I eventually got to the point when I could figure out ahead of time who would get cancer and who would not. Eventually after thousands of clients, I realized what I was looking at were the early warning markers not just for cancer but nearly all chronic diseases. If they were managed early enough, we could mitigate or turn off the disease conditions.

MARKERS OF CHRONIC DISEASE

Enclosed below is an overview of the major factors that we have found in different disease cases.

a) Hyperacidity – One of the primary causes of regulatory blockage is hyperacidity, defined as a significant decrease in the pH of the cellular environment. Most often hyperacidity is due to dietary indiscretions and overall dysfunction of the digestive and eliminative organs, as well as to the chronic stresses of our modern lifestyles.

b) Dysbiosis – An impaired digestive system with imbalanced bacteria flora is also a significant regulatory blockage, known as "dysbiosis." As Dr's. Astor & Swartz like to point out, the digestive system is really the fifth sensory organ, the system through which we experience our environment most directly – via the food we eat. When it's out of balance and unhealthy, "dysbiosis" occurs. This can be due to the following reasons:

1. Incorrect pH – When the GI tract is either hyperacidity or hypoacid (especially as we grow

older) it results in impaired digestion.

2. Leaky Gut Syndrome – This occurs when the intestinal
    lining, damaged by yeast, fungus, or fermentative
    bacteria, allows toxic material to leak through the
    intestinal wall (leaky gut syndrome), thereby decreasing
    the absorption of essential nutrients

3. Fungus, Parasites and Virus – The presence of
    unwanted microorganisms like candida albicans
    and parasites can affect the integrity of the GI
    tract. Once again, our diets, high in animal proteins
    and bad fats and low in fiber, are implicated in
    dysbiosis. Having a long-term viral infection can
    also grossly affect immunity.

4. Insufficient Good Bacteria – The overuse of
    antibiotics and steroids can badly upset the ecology
    of the gut leading to a reduction in good bacteria and
    a proliferation of bad microorganisms

5. Allergies – A third blockage is related to food
    intolerances, which set up immune reactions and
    lead to an overloaded lymphatic system, which
    then no longer distinguishes external threats, and
    so becomes ineffective in defending the body from
    infective agents.

6. Focal Disturbance Fields – Focal disturbance fields
    are another very important blockage to regulatory
    function. These are places in the body, called "foci,"
    that have sub clinical infection and/or inflammation
    and can act at a distance, usually along the vital
    energy meridian lines of the body, causing disease or
    dysfunction at another location.

Very often these foci occur in the head region, particularly in teeth. Impacted wisdom teeth, infected root canal-treated teeth, implants, metal fillings, crowns, bridges, and "cavitations" (incompletely healed bone from tooth extractions), can all cause problems further up or down their meridian lines. Rarely do these infections show up on a regular dental x-ray, nor are they felt; they are sub clinical and sub symptomatic. But the bacteria associated with focal sites can cause serious infections and disease in other parts of the body.

Focal disturbance fields can also be associated with non-dental implants, scars (both from surgery and from injuries), fractures, and other traumas to the body. While these injuries may seem completely healed, they may nonetheless be causing severe blockages along their particular meridians. Resolving these foci can sometimes bring instantaneous relief to a distant part of the body, as when an old scar on the hand is injected with a biological remedy and that person's migraines disappear; or when a root canal-treated tooth is removed and an ovarian cyst disappears.

Heavy Metal – A fifth type of blockage is heavy metal toxicity, primarily from metals used in dental fillings: mercury, tin, copper, zinc, silver and palladium (associated with gold fillings). Other heavy metal exposures may include lead, aluminum, cadmium, and nickel. Heavy metals wreak havoc with biological systems, acting as systemic poisons.

Drugs – Long-term chemotherapy and the use of allopathic medications such as antibiotics, corticoids, anti-rheumatics and anti-inflammatory drugs can also create regulatory problems.

Psychological Stress – Finally, long-term psychological stress can have serious impact on the overall regulatory ability of the body. Factors like divorce, the death of a family member, or some other emotional loss can often be a trigger that precipitates illness.

Organ Dysfunction – Either Hypoglycemia or Hyperglycemia are hidden health concerns that keep cropping up and need to be addressed. Relatively slight variations in hormonal levels can also have major clinical consequences.

Metabolic – Many people are suffering from an impaired Phase 2 liver detox pathway problem. When this is identified and corrected many attending health issues are resolved.

Vaccines – A significant degree of pediatric health concerns arise out of an impaired immune response to vaccine. There are specific methods to neutralize vaccine damage.

All of the before mentioned need to be assessed and treated. We have more that 15 years experience in screening for all these variables. We have clients who fly in from other South-East Asian countries to be assessed for these variables. Imagine what they discovered? After years of struggling with drugs, they started finding significant changes in their health. Thousands of people with common allergy conditions like asthma, eczema and chronic digestive issues have had their lives dramatically changed as a result of the Optimal Health System.

A senior executive who flew in from Bali to be assessed because she had treated a cancerous breast lump discovered in 40 minutes her dental filling had lead to her breast cancer. Someone who had a genetically related case of hypertriglyceridemia discovered that if he stopped eating wheat, his triglycerides would become normal. Eventually, I developed a sophisticated assessment system using software and hardware that would screen people for early warning markers of disease called "The Optimal Health System".

THE OPTIMAL HEALTH SYSTEM

The devices and tests that we use in the health assessment tap into the body's own data communication pathway. By monitoring the body's response to biochemistry, biophysics and biomechanical and emotional signals, it determines energy demands communication pathways and assists the practitioner in establishing a treatment protocol to bring the body back into balance. This highly individualized approach to wellness opens a new chapter in health science, introducing technology that bridges the gap between science and complementary medicine.

The software program then works out individualized solutions for nutrition, diet, exercise water levels and other appropriate interventions that could include supplements, bodywork and homoeopathics. By creating a personalized tailored coaching program we found we could change the health of thousands of individuals in a sustainable way. The Singapore government has just given us a grant to run a clinical study. Currently, this system has been launched in Singapore and is being launched in Malaysia and Thailand. We need not die before our time. Thousands of children need not lose their parents before their time. We can choose to truly live long and prosper.

by
Dr Sundardas D. Annamalay ND, PhD, MD(MA)
Naturopathic Physician, Acupuncturist, Homoeopath,
Clinical Nutritionist, NLP Trainer, Clinical Hypnotherapist

REFERENCES:

1. *The Random House Dictionary of the English Language. New York: Random House, Inc; 1969.*

2. *Bishop JE, Waldholz M. Genome. New York: Simon and Schuster; 1990.*

3. *Hesketh JE, Partridge K. Gene cloning: studies of nutritional regulation of gene expression. Proc Nutri Soc. 1996;55:575-581.*

4. *Motulsky, AG. Nutrition and genetic susceptibility to common diseases. Am J Clin Nutr. 1992;5S:1244-1245.*

5. *Baker SM. Detoxification and Healing. New Canaan, Conn: Keats Publishing, Inc; 1987.*

6. *Galland L. Medicine in Different Perspective: A Biographical Approach to Illnesses can erase the False Distinction between Science and Humanism in Medicine. 133 E 73 St. New York, NY 10021.*

7. *Bland JS. The use of complementary medicine for healthy aging. Alt Therapies. 1998;4(4):42-48.*

8. *Baker SM. Detoxification and Healing. New Canaan, Conn: Keats Publishing, Inc; 1987:173.*

9. *Williams R. The concept of genetotrophic disease. Lancet. 1950;1:287-289.*

10. *Perrine SP, Olivieri NF, Faller DV, Vichinsky EP, Dover GJ, Ginder GD. Butyrate derivatives. New agents for stimulating fetal globin production in the B-globin disorders. Am J Ped Hematol/Oncol. 1994;16(1):67-71.*

11. *Fries J, Crapo LM. Vitality and Aging. San Francisco, Calif: W.H. Freeman & Co; 1981.*

12. *Evans W, Rosenberg IH. Biomarkers. The 10 keys to Prolonging Vitality. New York: Fireside; 1991.*

13. *Fries JF. Aging, natural death, and the compression of morbidity. NEJM. 1980;303:130.*

14. *Murray CJL, Lopez AD. Alternative projections of mortality by cause 1990-2020: global burden of disease study. Lancet. 1997;349:1498-1504.*

15. *Bland JS. The use of complementary medicine for healthy aging. Alt Therapies. 1998;4(4):42.*

16. *Bland JS. Functional Medicine: Applications to Disorders of Gene Expression. Paper presented at: Fifth International Symposium on Functional Medicine; May 3-6, 1998; Hawaii.*

17. *Riggs KM, Spiro III A, Tucker K, Rush D. Relations of vitamin B-12, vitamin B-6, folate, and homocysteine to cognitive performance in the Normative Aging Study. Am J Clin Nutr. 1996;63:306-314.*

18. *Levin B. Nutritional Management of Inflammatory Disorders. Gig Harbor, Wash: Institute for Functional Medicine; 1998. 19. Obesity in Malaysia. Ismai,l MN, Chee SS, Nawawi H, Yusoff K, Lim TO, James WP.Department of Nutrition and Dietetics, University Kebangsaan Malaysia, Kuala, Lumpur. mismail@medic.ukm.my*

ABOUT SUNDARDAS

PhD (USA), ND (Aust., USA), MD (MA) (Sri Lanka), DABAAHP (USA)

Naturopathic Physician, Acupuncturist and Homoeopath, Clinical Nutritionist, Clinical Hypnotherapist

Dr. Sundardas is the leading Naturopathic Physician, practicing for the last 20 years in Singapore. His clinical interests include children's learning disabilities (ADD/ADHD, Autism, Infections), Allergies, Women's Health Concerns, Musculoskeletal Pain and Healthy Aging. He is currently Professor of Naturopathic Medicine at the Youngson Institute of Natural Science (Australia) and runs a busy practice in Singapore. He was also a visiting professor to the Open International University for Complementary Medicine (Sri Lanka).

Dr. Sundardas is a certified by the American Board of Anti-Aging Health Professionals and a member of the American Academy of Anti-Aging Medicine. He is also a registered Naturopathic Physician with the Naturopathic Practitioners' Association (Australia) and Fellow of the Faculty, University of Natural Medicine (Nevada).

His client list includes leading Asian actresses and entertainers, diplomats, ambassadors, political figures, royalty from Malaysia and wealthy families in Asia, the Middle East and India. Among other clients are executives from Goldman and Sachs, IBM, SIMEX, FOREX, companies like Batey Ads, Business Trends, NTUC, as well as, local government bodies like the Ministry of Defense and Ministry of Education (Singapore).

He is the CEO of Sundardas Naturopathic Clinic, which specializes in the management of chronic health conditions.

Dr. Sundardas is a speaker, trainer and consultant to health-related companies and has served as a wellness and nutritional consultant to companies in Singapore, Thailand and India. Dr. Sundardas has helped companies in wellness areas to generate more than $15 million dollars in sales using strategic technical positioning.

Dr. Sundardas is a well-respected media personality who has been interviewed by TCS, CNBC Asia and BBC World and others for the last

19 years. He has been interviewed many times on radio and ran a regular talk show for two years on Complementary Medicine. He is the author of 18 books eight of which have been published.

He has won awards both local and foreign ranging from Associate of the Teachers' Network awarded by the Ministry of Education (Singapore) to Dr. Yudvir Singh Memorial Award (India) to being listed in the *Who's Who of Intellectuals* (USA).

His company Natural Therapies Research Centre recently won the Promising SME 500 Award. Promising SME 500 Award is one of the reputable awards in Singapore initiated by the Small Medium Business Association (SMBA), to recognize and acknowledge promising small and medium business enterprises in recognition of company achievements, good business practices, operational efficiency, leadership, sustainability, value and use of modern technology to create for customers, the firm and its partners.

Dr. Sundardas is a national and international speaker and trainer on wellness, peak performance and sustainability and has shared the stage with the likes of Robert Kiyosaki, Tom Wheelwright, Ken McElroy, Rick Belluzo, and Krish Dhanam at events like the National Achiever's Congress. He is available to do talks and keynote speeches.

CHAPTER 11

BUILDING THE WILDLY SUCCESSFUL YOU

THE CLARITY OF PURPOSE

BY JOE ORSAK

SUCCESS

*He has achieved success
who has lived well,
laughed often, and loved much;
who has enjoyed the trust of pure women,
the respect of intelligent men
and the love of little children;
who has filled his niche
and accomplished his task;
who has left the world better than he found it*

*whether by an improved poppy,
a perfect poem, or a rescued soul;
who has never lacked appreciation of
Earth's beauty
or failed to express it;
who has always looked for the best in others
and given them the best he had;
whose life was an inspiration;
whose memory a benediction.*

The above is often attributed to Ralph Waldo Emerson. After a little homework and some diligent use of Google, I believe it is properly attributed to Bessie Stanley who passed in 1952. The poem first appeared in 1904 as a submission for a contest held in *Brown Book Magazine* by George Livingston Richards Co. of Boston, Massachusetts. It hangs on the wall in my mother's office as a gift to her from me some many years ago. It has been a wonderful guiding philosophy for me over the years, and I find it ever so relevant, even now, as I begin to lay down these pages about what I feel to be a key component in being a success in life, namely clarity of purpose. While I will use religious references, and while I certainly possess a deep faith, these are by no means necessary to understand the power of the topic. Let's dig in!

It was roughly 30AD. The ruling religious teachers of Jerusalem had just tested Jesus of Nazareth. They had asked him for a sign that would convince them of his authority. He flatly denied them and alluded to his death and resurrection as the only sign that they would receive. They lacked the required clarity to see and interpret the signs that had already been provided and would certainly miss it should Jesus have granted them the opportunity for another. Jesus retired to the city of Caesarea Philippi, an ancient Roman city, located at the southwestern base of Mount Hermon, which is located in between today's Syria and Lebanon. It was from this day forward that Jesus would begin teaching his disciples about his necessary death and subsequent resurrection. He needed his disciples to understand their calling and to have clarity of purpose.

Jesus spoke to his disciples and asked them a question of clarity. "Who do people say that the Son of Man is?" (For clarity sake Jesus referred to himself as the Son of Man, which is topic for another time.) In short, Jesus was asking who people thought he was. His disciples responded, "Some say John the Baptist, and others, Elijah; but still others, Jeremiah, or one of the prophets."

Knowing that the masses lacked clarity, he asked further and more pointedly, "But who do you say that I am?" It was Simon who piped up with the answer. "You are the Christ, the Son of the living God." And for this clear and accurate response Jesus answered, "Blessed are you, Simon Barjona, because flesh and blood did not reveal this to you, but My Father who is in heaven. I also say to you that you are Peter, and upon this rock I will build My church; and the gates of Hades will not overpower it." (Matthew 16:13-18)

I hope to avoid boring you with too many Greek words and definitions, but it's very important that you understand this. The term Church was never intended be construed as a place. The word "church" in the New Testament is translated from the Greek word 'ekklesia' which comes from two words 'ek' meaning 'out' and 'kaleo' meaning to 'call.' An *ekklesia* or "calling out" is more than just an assembly. There are numerous other Greek words that can all mean an assembly. The word ekklesia, however, was a political term rather than a religious term. Jesus chose this word with great purpose. (3)

When pilot asked Jesus if he was the king of the Jews, Jesus responded, "Yes, it is as you say." (Luke 23:3). Jesus was the King and appropriately chose a political term to represent his and his father's summoning of those who had been called out of their homes and their lives for his purpose. In classical Greek, "ekklesia" meant "an assembly of citizens summoned by the crier, the legislative assembly." Jesus was going to build his called out assembly on the singular clarity of who he was, "The Christ…" (whose purpose was to die for the sins of the world) "…the Son of the living God."

I want to avoid a sermon, as my intent is certainly otherwise. So, stick with me. While as a believer in Jesus, I certainly have my convictions about faith in Jesus, but my intent here is solely to share my message regarding the clarity of purpose. I intend to convey only the amazing inspirational power we possess as humans when we have clarity of purpose.

When this scene unfolded, from that day forward Jesus taught his disciples that his purpose as Christ and Son of the living God was to die and three days later to resurrect. It took his disciples some time to come to terms with this simple message. In fact, when Peter chastised Jesus about this notion and said that he wished Jesus' death would never happen, Jesus called him Satan. (Matthew 16:22-23) Do you think Jesus had clarity of purpose? Despite seeing the coming events that would unfold for him (beating, whipping, crucifixion and public mocking), which resulted in the medical condition known as hematidrosis (sweating blood), even at the sheer thought of those events, he still understood with perfect clarity what his calling was and knew the importance of sharing that very clear message.

Once Jesus' disciples grasped this message it would become a message that would change the world, as we know it. It was clarity of purpose and calling that gave the disciples passion, strength and voice to do just that. Twelve men, largely, uneducated fisherman, tax collectors, etc., turned the world upside down. After Jesus' resurrection, twelve men had one voice with one message. "He is risen." It is a message that is celebrated all around the world each Easter and over 2 billion plus people resonate with that message today. Clarity of purpose! The clarity of the called! Let that sink in for a second. There are **TWO BILLION PLUS** believers in that simple message. Twelve mostly uneducated men, who all were willing to face horrible death for the clarity of their purpose, changed the world. You can change the world too. The potential is within each of us. Once we connect to our purpose we are fueled by the passion that ignites from that connection.

I want to point out one last noteworthy thing. Did Jesus understand that when his disciples gained their clarity of purpose that they would be able to succeed beyond what they themselves ever could grasp? Do you remember this phrase? "…and the gates of Hades will not overpower it." Gates are DEFENSIVE tools rather than OFFENSIVE weapons. No one ever saw a soldier march on to the field of battle with a gate in his hand. Gates DEFEND. Jesus wanted to make clear that when his disciples possessed the necessary clarity, the very gates of Hades would be unable to stand in defense against them. In clarity of purpose there is tremendous power. They, with the power of clarity of purpose, would be marching into the strongholds of Hades; and those strongholds would be powerless to stand against the message they shared. Make no mistake about it!

I have had the good fortune to study a number of different business coaching and personal development courses. One thing that I have come to realize is that all, in some way or another, start at the same point. They often, however, approach it from different angles. It is this that I alluded to at the beginning of this chapter. I hope to provide yet another look at the same thing. I do this, simply, because I feel I have another angle, rather than because I feel I have a better view, or because of a lack in other material. It is my hope that sharing this vantage point will allow you clarity on an otherwise unclear, yet ultimately important, concept.

With Stephen Covey, clarity is the process of developing your "personal mission statement," which is based in Habit 2 (begin with the end in mind). With Michael Gerber, employing E-myth knowledge is the process of developing your "primary aim" and your companies "strategic objective." With Tom Fleming of the Referral Institute and his "Certified Networker" material, clarity of purpose is the development of your emotional-based marketing message. With Steve Stinek, through his most excellent book, it is called "Start with Why." None of these individuals lack in their material. They have fantastic insight, and I would encourage you to study ALL of their material, if only to provide more insight into this single subject. YOU MUST, MUST, MUST, possess the clarity of your calling – the clarity of purpose. Call it your primary aim, your mission statement, your emotional-based marketing message, your "why," or in my terms, your clarity of purpose. Call it whatever you wish, but you MUST begin with it.

I am a huge fan of each of these men's material on the subject. Each has spent a huge quantity of their lives developing their work and each has been foundational to my understanding of this material. I owe them a great debt of gratitude for pulling out of me the clarity of purpose. Purpose is something that exists in each of us, but the clarity OF that purpose is rare to find.

Most people will tell you that they are unaware of their purpose in life – their calling. Look at the world around us, and it is easy to conclude that the world is filled with people who move through each day reacting to a seemingly random series of events until they wake no more. What a BLEAK existence. I am here to tell you that you already KNOW what your purpose is, but you simply lack the clarity OF that purpose. I am here to tell you that if you dig into this concept you can find your clarity of purpose; and each day from that point forward, you can possess a life filled with passion and excitement. When you have clarity of purpose, everything simply makes more sense. When you have clarity of purpose, you are energized and equipped with the fuel necessary to build the wildly successful you!

ABOUT JOE

Joe Orsak is the Chief Marketing Officer and a previous talk radio host for one of the fastest growing credit restoration companies in the United States. The company has grown at a rate of over three hundred percent for the last three years and achieved the rank of *Consumer Voted #1* in Texas for 2010 and 2011 consecutively. Orsak is frequently sought for speaking engagements on radio and in person on the topic of the power of obtaining clarity of purpose for building a wildly successful business.

As an ordained minister trained in psychology and marketing, Orsak brings a unique approach to the concept of building a wildly successful business. The approach is based on practical experience and previous successes. Happily married for nearly two decades and a father of two, he understands the power of balance and foundation in tapping into the power of purpose and applying it to all areas of life for extreme fulfillment.

CHAPTER 12

7 STEPS TO LEVERAGE WITH CAN

BY JOSH McWHORTER

Before you read on thinking you're learning the latest and greatest tricks of Wall Street, let me warn you – you're not. Before you read on thinking that this is another piece blasting Wall Street for the tricks of the past, let me warn you – it's not. For most of us, some anonymous money manager sitting in a towering office overlooking the busy streets of Manhattan rarely predicates financial success. In fact, financial success lies within the pathways of our body between our heart and mind. Those of you who are able to look past the haze of the crowd, ground out the noise we call *wisdom*, and avoid the countless traps of expert's opinions *can* enjoy financial success and leverage that success for the enjoyment of countless others.

Let me start with my *why*. Why? Why get up in the morning? Why go to work? Why do countless other things? I found myself pondering that very question. I still contemplate *why*, but I had some of the greatest professionals take time out of their schedule to guide me along my path. Before I founded Black Oak Asset Management, I was with a big firm where I excelled to running a very successful investment platform at a community bank. In 3 years being in the lead role at Black Oak, we've successfully added new staff members, grown assets we manage by tens of millions of dollars, and revenue has increased over 100%. I found myself wanting more and not being completely satisfied. I turned to real estate deals to broaden my horizons and test theory. By all accounts, that has been a success too. What I found was Black Oak was created to give me the financial freedom to make a difference in the community I serve. Yes, I want to provide for my family. Yes, I would like to make money. However, that was only a small part. I firmly believe my family and I will be fine. I firmly believe I'll make enough money. More importantly, I was given by the grace of God a tool, known by many as Black Oak, to create a positive change by leveraging our resources to create a positive change. Life has never been clearer. In the end, I found that I wanted to take on like-minded clients who wanted to worry less about their money and its limitations and more about what they want and how they can also create positive change within our community.

So, how does this actually translate into financial success? It's been my experience when you, as a client, walk in to see an advisor, whether it be financial, tax or legal related, you're immediately given all the many reasons of what you *can't* do based on your resources. Therefore, when you leave you're generally feeling that if you don't do this or don't do that, you'll scrape by in order to do some of the things you desire. You're less likely to give the extra dollar or the extra hour of your time out of fear of running out. Let me challenge you to think about what you *can* do. How do you do that? Before reading these steps, please realize that I'm talking to a longer term investor who spends less than what he or she makes and does so in order to leverage financial results to benefit their community.

STEP 1 – Create your SMART goals. Think about it ... is it easier to plan for retirement at 65 or an income of $5,000/ mo to last to infinity, $100,000 to your favorite charity, and $500,000 to your family in the event of an untimely death within the next 10 years? Your goals should be specific, measurable, achievable, realistic and timely. Once you know your goals, you're now able to quantify what it will take to get there. Also, you're less likely to make the extra purchase that you don't need – that only gets you in trouble. In determining your goals, it will become apparent what's important to you. You'll discover your *why*.

STEP 2 – Create a plan. Let's assume your goals are the aforementioned income, charity and family needs listed above. Factoring in realistic returns on investments, assumptions on taxes/inflation and what you can actually put toward your goal, you can see whether or not your goals are realistic. I suggest using worst-case scenarios such as low investment returns, tax increases, inflation at higher than average rates and less than favored health. If you're successful in that environment, imagine yourself when investments do better than expected or tax rates and inflation are lower.

STEP 3 – Monitor your plan. How many times have you created a plan, for anything, and it worked out as planned – most of the time – never. It's important to know that plans change, evolve or *completely* change. New investment products come on the market, tax polices change and monetary policy changes. Therefore, you may get ahead of your goals or behind, but consistent measurement of those goals will often affect the outcome.

STEP 4 – Giving in your plan. Why in the world would you give when you're hardly getting by, or why would you give if you have more than enough, but are worried about markets, taxes, longevity, etc.? I have no proof, other than close to a decade of working with clients and observing that financial success correlates with giving. Now, we have the chicken and egg argument. Did the success come after giving or was giving a byproduct of success? Most, I've noticed, gave very early on. You can make the argument from scripture that states that God blesses those who bless others or God blesses those who are responsible with His gifts. I'm not going to debate whether that should be giving directly to God through your church or giving to charity. It's a question of the heart. Giving, itself, is a gift. It can hurt, almost to the point of pain; but those who give, generally receive. Going down the religious road, in Malachi 3:10, God says to "Test me in this way." Many scholars debate the text and whether or not God actually intends for us to test him. The ironic thing to me is that through many centuries and translations, it's the only place in the Bible where we're instructed to test Him. I want to add that I don't believe just because you give, you will receive money. There are so many other blessings that come from giving, too many to list, that I encourage you, give.

STEP 5 – Worry less about investment returns. We want to worry less about our financial future. I've read reports and studies that dictate greater success with less worry. When you worry less about the returns, you start thinking about the change you can make. How, with the markets we've seen, is this possible? Let's go back to 9th grade geometry where we learned about something called a bell shaped curve. It was that crazy predictor of distributions that looked like a bell! Go back as far as you can with the stock market returns and graph the results. Crazy, isn't?! If we assume the laws of geometry are correct, we can protect ourselves from a worst case scenario. How? Let's assume that we have a 2.5% chance of a 50% or greater loss. If changing your investment mix is directed by the results and you believe that asset allocation is greatest indicator of future returns, why take the unneeded risk of being overly weighted in stocks? Yes, as absurd as it sounds, a stock guy is telling you not to own as much stock as you can. I found, in general, clients are invested more aggressively than they really want to be. When I started in this business I was given a *risk tolerance questionnaire* that asked 10 questions; it was supposed to accurately tell me whether or not a person was conservative, moderate or aggressive. I laugh when I think about that sheet. What a wall street trick! History has shown market timing, stock picking, etc has rarely translated into long term success. But, you need the market in order to gain returns to accomplish your goals. Take as much risk as you can afford, but not a penny more. Use things like correlation coefficients to gain an idea of what your portfolio would look like assuming negative and positive returns. By doing this, you'll start to worry less about your money. You'll worry less the next time a *talking head* comes on TV to tell you the market is heading for a crash. You'll worry less the next time you read about a pending blow up in the financial markets.

STEP 6 – Create the change. By now, you've written goals, which can be liberating in itself. You've created the plan for obtaining your goals. You've started testing and monitoring the plan, and you now have the right allocation that will allow you to worry less about returns. Now, you're able to think about how you want to spend the excess money and time you now know you possess. Is it a charity? Is it a church or other religious organization? Do you want to take kids to the park? Do you want clean up roads? Do you want to support college bound students to aid them in receiving their degrees? Whatever you're *why*, do it! Some of you may have trouble coming up with your *why*. If you're fortunate enough to be married, ask your spouse what makes you tick. Some expert advice given to me was to ask Vanessa, my wife. I learned there were several things that made me who I am, and I found several things about myself interesting. Whatever yours is, you now know what you can do and how much of it you can do.

STEP 7 – Leverage. "From everyone who has been given much, much will be demanded; and from the one who has been entrusted with much, much more will be asked" Luke 12:48. God demands us to be stewards of His money and resources. If you're reading this book, I'm going to venture out on a strong limb and assume you've been blessed. How are you leveraging your blessings toward others? First, and maybe the better question is, how do you leverage your blessings toward others? "And everyone who has left houses or brothers or sisters or father or mother or children or fields for my sake will receive a hundred times as much and will inherit eternal life" Matthew 19:29. Whether this passage was intended to be taken literally or not can be discussed all day. The truth is: by giving of your resources you have already leveraged! I've been in this business for close to a decade, and I have yet to see any money manager who has provided that kind of return. Let's assume that after all the things you want to accomplish, you have an extra $20 per month to give. That $20 puts a few hot meals in front of a child who wouldn't have eaten otherwise. That child may one day realize the only reason they are where they are is because someone gave them a meal that allowed them to maintain focus in school, propelling them to a position of great financial success where they meet the needs of 20 children per month – all because you gave $20. Maybe you were given the gift of many fruitful relationships. You may not have the monetary funds at present to give further; but when you share the vision you have with others, you will be shocked at the response of your friends. Through your vision maybe a few will realize they can do more, and in doing so, hundreds of lives will improve.

I want to end with a story about what we're planning. Money is the leading cause of divorce in this country. If your checkbook isn't balanced, neither will your marriage. You've probably heard the expression in sports: "Together we stand, divided we fall." That resonates with money and marriage. Therefore with an assist from my trusted advisors, Black Oak is planning an event of ages that will cost us plenty and net us almost nothing. As you read, remember my *why* and that will help you understand why my firm and I are doing this. Black Oak is simply a tool to create positive change in the community we serve. We're planning a money management course as an overnight stay at the top hotel in our community. We're inviting married couples that are serious about changing their course of direction for the benefit of themselves and their community. We're hosting as many couples as we can accommodate for a dinner, a seminar that evening on three principles of money management, a free overnight stay to rediscover their spouse and their finances, and a breakfast at no cost to them.

I have no idea what hosting the course will cost, nor am I worried. My only worry is that couples that need to be there won't be able to attend that night or there will be too many couples to host all who want to come. Principles such as spending less than what you make, committing to goals, etc will be shared, nothing more. Many will say and are saying you can't do it. Many will say and are saying it's too expensive. Many will say and are saying you're crazy! That's the world's view of this way of thinking. Fortunately, for me, I live for a greater purpose. This is my *why*. This is a way I can take the resources I've been given and affect positive change within the community I serve. This is how I leverage resources through *can*.

ABOUT JOSH

Starting his career with Capstone Financial in 2003, Josh McWhorter earned "Rising Leaders" status in his first four months with the firm. This was a first in the firm's history. McWhorter went on to work with a community bank, serving as the lead investment advisor for individual clients, growing that business 900% in three years. In March 2009, McWhorter founded Black Oak. In three years time, Black Oak has grown to nine team members and has been featured in The AJC, SmartMoney, Market-Watch, US News & World Report and CBS 46 of Atlanta.

WcWhorter wanted to be more than an advisor. He wanted to positively affect the communities he served by leveraging time, money and relationships. More important than growth and accolades, the vision of what Black Oak would become is being realized. McWhorter continues to serve on numerous committees at his church, Cartersville First Baptist, and also serves on the board for Advocates for Children. Black Oak supports Advocates for Children, Bartow County Women's Resource Center, The Etowah Scholarship Foundation and The Good Neighbor Homeless Shelter, only to name a few.

CHAPTER 13

FINDING FINANCIAL SECURITY IN VOLATILE TIMES:

SAFE RETIREMENT PLANNING

BY ALLEN NEUENSCHWANDER

When 2008's Wall Street meltdown took down Main Street, a lot of ordinary people saw their retirement funds shrink in a way they never thought possible. Even now, global economic volatility and U.S. government gridlock continue to threaten our financial security, even as the largest group of Americans in history is headed towards retirement age.

That's why proper planning for the golden years is more essential than ever.

This is an incredibly important subject for me; I know firsthand how a family's financial security can be shattered – because it happened to mine. I had earned my MBA in Finance, completed my CPA certification, worked four years in public accounting, and had just started my own business, when my dad and daughter were killed simultaneously in a tragic car accident.

That left my mother with three young kids at home to take care of by herself and with a second major shock still to come – my father no longer had a life insurance policy! Unbeknownst to all of us, he had taken some bad advice and cancelled his policy, leaving almost nothing for my mom to live on.

As I forged ahead, dealing with estate settlement and wrongful death lawsuits in the aftermath of the accident and trying to put together a future for the rest of my family, I came to realize that many others were hit with these kinds of unexpected crises – and, incredibly, were totally unprepared for them. If they had had good ongoing financial advice from someone who had the skills and knowledge to help safeguard their future, the difference to their lives would have been an amazingly positive one.

That inspired me to start an entirely new career. I embarked on a two year advanced training program and became a Certified Financial Planner ™.

And I'm very happy I did. When I started in this field in 1986, I thought things couldn't get any crazier in the financial world than when the Dow Jones plunged over 500 points in one day. Now, I look back at that time with some nostalgia, because today's economic uncertainty makes that brief disruption look like a minor blip.

In this chapter, I'd like to discuss the reasons why today's economic outlook is so uncertain – and why you need to begin planning for your financial security today, no matter how young or old you may be. Finally, I'll provide some solid advice on how you can approach this daunting challenge.

AMERICA – ASLEEP AT THE ECONOMIC WHEEL?

We've seen on the news the economic carnage that's been created in Greece, because of their incredible debt levels and entitlement programs as well as the population's inability to face fiscal realities. Frankly, I have those concerns about our country; there's long-term cause for concern both for the U.S. economy and the financial outlook for both current and future retirees.

Over the past 60 years, the American Retirement has had as its foundation a "three- legged stool," which you can see pictured below:

This stool has as its legs: Social Security, Corporate Pension Programs and Personal Savings. Unfortunately, the first two of these legs are cracked and the third has its share of splintering as well.

Let's look more closely at them.

STOOL LEG #1: SOCIAL SECURITY

On April 23 2012 the Social Security Board of Trustees annual report press release warned that Social Security would be unable to meet its obligations by 2033. And you can't even trust that prediction; it was recently moved *forward* three years due to increasing costs and lower revenues.

These deficits will have to be addressed with solutions that will be difficult and unpopular. To maintain the promised benefits, eligibility ages must be raised substantially and means-testing will be put into effect; that would mean those seniors who have substantial assets or income may get far less Social Security benefits – or none at all.

STOOL LEG #2: PENSION PLANS

Company pension plans are rapidly going the way of the dinosaur. Many of those still offered by some employers are seriously under funded; and the government agency that's supposed to provide back-up for them, the PBGC (Pension Benefit Guaranty Corporation), doesn't have anywhere near enough money to cover multiple large bankruptcies. Many companies that offered 401(k) savings plans as a pension alternative discontinued them or stopped matching contributions in 2011. In addition, because state and local governments have been so cash-starved in recent years, many generous state and municipal employee plans are being slashed or terminated.

STOOL LEG #3: PERSONAL SAVINGS

Many Baby Boomers, raised in the post-World War II era of affluence, have been conspicuous consumers, spending more than they save, incurring massive amounts of personal debt, and pursuing a "show it all and owe it all" lifestyle. The country's recent economic woes have only worsened the situation with many Boomers now hoping to work until the age of seventy, versus the traditional retirement ages of sixty-two or sixty-five – or they find themselves unable to afford to retire at all.

According to a February 19, 2011 article in *The Wall Street Journal*, "the median household headed by a person aged 60 to 62 with a 401(k) account has *less than one-quarter of what is needed* in that account to maintain its standard of living in retirement."

OUR SICK MEDICAL SYSTEM

Unfortunately, the future financial pain doesn't even stop with our three-legged stool, because medical costs are skyrocketing just at the point where Medicare, like Social Security, is running out of time and money. The same study that forecast Social Security going broke in 2033 has Medicare heading for the same kind of trouble nine years earlier – in 2024. Again, obvious, necessary, and unpopular solutions – delaying benefits, rationing of health care, and means-testing – will have to be considered.

As for President Obama's Affordable Care Act, it's composed of 2,700 pages of largely unfunded or under funded mandates that attempt to provide free medical coverage to the uninsured – by requiring that *everyone* have medical insurance. Congress will have to take steps to get rid of the red ink. This program creates major uncertainty for businesses and has helped limit economic growth by stifling the hiring of additional workers.

ECONOMIC STORM CLOUDS

Beyond the potential breakdown of critical financial support systems for seniors, the overall economic climate has a lot of storm clouds forming that could severely affect traditional retirement strategies. For example:

EUROPEAN RECESSION & UNCERTAINTY

It's clear that the crisis in Europe is far from over. They're currently experiencing a "double dip" recession, as Greece's and Spain's ongoing debt problems continue to threaten the Euro currency. All of this turmoil will only have a minor long-term impact on America; however, overblown reporting from the media on this topic will most certainly cause stock market volatility on Wall Street.

THE TAX CLIFF

The Wall Street Journal has referred to the end of the 2012 tax year as the "Tax Cliff." Many tax breaks expire then and much higher individual tax rates will automatically kick in, which could end up costing all of America's small businesses around $240 billion. Estate taxes will also skyrocket, depending on what Congress does.

Since real tax and entitlement program overhaul will take months (if not years), expect Congress to enact only short term solutions in 2012 and early 2013 to delay the pending crisis.

DRAMATIC RISE IN INTEREST RATES

The Fed can only keep interest rates artificially low for the short-term. As the U. S. economy eventually accelerates or foreign citizens regain confidence and reposition much of their savings out of U.S. dollars, interest rates will rise rapidly and heavy inflation could result from the excess supply of U.S. dollars caused by the massive spending on the Government's Troubled Asset Relief Program (TARP).

CONTINUED WALL STREET MYOPIA

Wall Street profited handsomely from the real estate bubble and poured kerosene on the fire by repackaging bad loans into high yield products sold globally and by aggressive high-profit market hedging activities. We all know the sad result. Until the huge U.S. (and international) financial institutions put traditional retail and commercial banking ahead of their high-profit, high-risk practices, job creation and the economy could once again be the ultimate victims.

BEYOND WALL STREET: THE WAY TO A SAFER FINANCIAL FUTURE

Despite all this gloom and doom, there are secure strategies all of us can pursue to both protect our "nest eggs" and build those funds to see us through our retirement years.

That starts with taking personal responsibility for our financial decisions and retirement security – and expecting less from the government. The most dependable and predictable helping hand for a more secure future is the one at the end of your own sleeve! Most people don't worry about retirement until it's far too late. They fail to educate themselves properly about investments or hire the proper financial advisors to help them see through the fog of uncertainty.

The first major lesson that needs to be learned is that stocks are *not* where you should be investing all your money. Longer-term bonds are extremely dangerous in an ultra-low interest rate environment. Wall Street, however, has a tremendous interest in influencing you to do just that. The brokerage firms want to encourage investment in securities because they make money both on individual transactions and on managing portfolios. That means the more activity you initiate, the more profits go in their pocket.

It's not just Wall Street pushing the individual investor in this direction – it's also the financial media, which is hugely biased toward securities and stock trading in order to make money from advertisers who sell securities products. As the 2008 downturn proved, their reporting and forecasting are often completely off the mark. Since the financial media is not held liable for the accuracy of their opinions nor the damage done by their advice, they are free to be as reckless as they want.

Bottom line? Until the media is honest about its financial reporting, and until banks and brokerage houses put the investors' needs first and dedicate themselves to fiduciary responsibility, bank and wire house broker recommendations are highly suspect, if not absolutely dangerous, to your financial future!

SECURE SOLUTIONS

The good news is there are independent investment advisors out there who *do* accept fiduciary responsibility, putting their clients' needs first. They are dedicated to creating the best balance between security and portfolio growth to ensure a safe and profitable retirement. I'm proud to call myself one of them.

In general, my advice to clients begins with suggesting that retirees keep at least two years worth of after-tax cost-of-living money in very low volatility income investments. That means that if a big bear market hits and stock prices plunge, they will have enough funds on hand to live off of that will remain safe from temporary market disruptions. They will be able to comfortably ride out the storm – without having to tap into long-term assets that may simultaneously be taking a huge short-term hit.

I also advise partial investment in insurance products. *Legal reserve life insurance companies have high percentage capital requirements, are regulated by the state insurance commission of every state in which they operate, and generally limit their investment risks by using reinsurors to protect against any possible catastrophic losses.* The insurance industry offers several alternative investments including some that now offer new "income for life" guarantees * to take the place of the corporate pension plans of old – and yet (unlike traditional pensions) they provide residual value to heirs.

Insurance products may have several powerful advantages over traditional investments. Some offer very competitive guarantees * on rates of return without any loss of principal. Some can set up a joint income for life during retirement. That's why, more and more, they are becoming the "safe harbor" of choice for a major portion of retirement investments.

These are rather sophisticated products, so potential investors should seek a competent advisor to help them analyze what products are available in their state, the financial strength of the issuer, what best suits their needs, and of course read the prospectus or offering documents.

Generally, I will advise a client to focus on a mix of traditional investments together with these guaranteed * insurance products. Of course, I don't provide a one-size-fits-all strategy for everyone; instead, I dedicate myself to providing customized solutions for each individual, depending on what stage of life they're in and what specific resources and goals they have.

> *Any Comments regarding safe and secure investments and, and guaranteed income streams refer only to fixed insurance products. They do not refer, in any way to securities or investment advisory products. Fixed insurance and annuity product guarantees are subject to the claims-paying ability of the issuing company and are not covered by Global Financial Private Capital or GF Investment Services.*

WHAT TO LOOK FOR IN A FINANCIAL COACH

Every major athlete, of course, uses the best coaches to push him or her to the next level of achievement. The right coach creates the conditions for success by objectively assessing the athlete's current status and then working on what's required to move forward to reach desired outcomes.

Financial coaches are no different. Their expertise and experience help individuals avoid serious investment mistakes, improve portfolio growth, and avoid unnecessary risk. And, obviously, it's critical to make the right choice when it comes to your financial coach. The financial advisor you used in your 30s and 40s for accumulation is unlikely to be well suited to guide you in the preservation and distribution stages of life.

So which financial coach is right for you? Here are a few factors to consider in your search:

Does the coach have real and relevant credentials?

Look for these titles in particular:

Certified Financial Planner ™ (CFP®)
Chartered Financial Consultant (ChFC), or
CPA Personal Financial Planning specialist (CPA PFS)

Credentials can provide some evidence of competence, but years of relevant experience are a key indicator.

Is the coach participating in substantial continuing education in his or her field?

In these volatile and fast-changing times, every financial coach should continue to review the latest research, consider the latest theories and expand his or her horizons so the best and most knowledgeable service can be provided.

What's the focus of their practice?

You'll want someone who has years of experience working predominately with clients who are in the preservation and distribution stages of their lives. Creating low-risk income, rather than risking a large negative sequence of returns with volatile growth oriented investments, is the key.

How credible is the coach?

You should review coaches' websites and other promotional materials to discover as much as you can about them, their philosophy, and how they present themselves. Of course, you can't just rely on their promotional material. Check state and federal regulatory websites for any disciplinary history.

How do you personally connect with the coach?

Once you've made a preliminary pick, call the finalist and arrange a complimentary appointment to discuss your goals and their processes. You can see if you're comfortable discussing personal information with the coach, if you can get candid responses to your questions, and you can then determine whether his or her approach resonates with you.

If you'd like a free consumer guide to finding the best financial coach for your needs, we have one available on our website at "http://www.outlookwealth.com/freereports". In the meantime, I wish you all the best for your future, as well as a pleasurable and prosperous retirement.

Allen Neuenschwander CPA, CFP®
Outlook Wealth Advisors, LLC
2002 Timberloch, Suite 120
The Woodlands, TX 77380

281.872.1515

Securities offered through GF Investment Services, LLC. Member FINRA/SIPC. Investment Advisory Services offered through Global Financial Private Capital, LLC an SEC Registered Investment Advisor.

Opinions expressed are those of the author, and not necessarily endorsed by GF Investment Services, LLC or Global Financial Private Capital, LLC.

ABOUT ALLEN

Allen Neuenschwander obtained a Bachelor Degree from Spring Hill College in Mobile, Alabama and a MBA from the University of Tennessee. He became a Certified Public Accountant, served as a Finance Officer during the Vietnam War and worked for four years in public accounting. A tragic accident caused him to become a Certified Financial Planner™ and redirect his life while living in Houston Texas. In his role as a financial planner, he aids clients with every area of finance, including financial and insurance planning, investment management and estate planning. He has served on the Board of Directors of the Houston Financial Planning Association (FPA) and the Investment Committee of the Houston Chapter of CPAs. Allen has been awarded the prestigious 5 Star Wealth Manager Award and will be recognized in the September 2012 edition of *Texas Monthly Magazine*. His hobbies include boating, snow skiing and working out. His office and residence are in The Woodlands, Texas.

Allen Neuenschwander CPA, CFP®
Outlook Wealth Advisors, LLC
2002 Timberloch, Suite 120
The Woodlands, TX 77380

281.872.1515

Securities offered through GF Investment Services, LLC. Member FINRA/SIPC. Investment Advisory Services offered through Global Financial Private Capital, LLC an SEC Registered Investment Advisor.

Opinions expressed are those of the author, and not necessarily endorsed by GF Investment Services, LLC or Global Financial Private Capital, LLC.

CHAPTER 14

RETIRING RICH WITHOUT THE WALL STREET BULL

BY EDDIE OVERDYKE

I was not a normal child. Even in the early teen years, I read the *Wall Street Journal* and the business section of the Atlanta paper whenever I could get my hands on it. I loved staying in hotels where the *USA Today* was delivered, just to get more information from the stock market section.

I built my nest egg via some of the more traditional methods of summer jobs and mini-entrepreneurial ventures, but I was so obsessed with building a foundation and starting early that I was known to pocket food money my parents gave me to eat with friends and instead made a couple of peanut butter and jelly and sandwiches.

Over the years, my little nest egg in the bank didn't earn a lot of interest; so, I decided the market was place. After all, conventional wisdom said I needed to be in the market. So, I headed out to find the best manager to pick the hottest stocks and to decide when to get in and out of the market. After all, I was finishing high school and on my way to college; I didn't have time for that.

I reached out to a broker at one of the big Wall Street firms and sent him around $5,000. That was a tremendous amount of money to me at the time, considering the car I was driving at the time cost $2,500 (my investment was double the price of my car as a high schooler!).

Fast-forward 4 years. I was home from college for the summer and opened a letter from the big Wall Street firm hoping to see big gains…instead it was a notice that the account balance was no longer high enough to pay the account fees, so please send more money.

Yep, in a short amount of time, market losses and account fees ate up my investment.

That incident led me back to school where my area of focus in my finance studies was the underperformance of Wall Street's traditional mutual funds and how they get away with it – a topic too long and too boring for this book, but deep down inside we know its true.

When I share my beginnings with most people they are shocked and appalled, but I view it as one of the least expensive lessons of my life. I found out in my early 20's what so many people find out in their 50's or 60's…the status quo that Wall Street has touted for so long: "Let our experts have your money, and we can pick the best stocks and time the market," just isn't the path of financial security.

So, I began my crusade to protect people from the misgivings of Wall Street.

The 3 Things You Must Know to Retire Rich:

1. Ending the Status Quo

    "Status Quo, you know, that is Latin for the mess we're in." – Ronald Reagan

Let's start with some of the traditional *status quo,* conventional wisdom that is so often broadcasted to unassuming hardworking Americans:

- Max out your 401(k) contributions.

- The stock market is the best place to put savings to earn a high rate of return.

- Wall Street's *expert* market timers and stock pickers can earn you a high rate of return.

- Buy term and invest the difference.

- Defer taxes until later.

Now, according to the Social Security Administration, out of 100 people turning age 65 today, only four are financially secure (with incomes of $35,000 or more). The other 96 are either relying on family, charity or still required to work.

Knowing this alone, it should be no surprise to you to hear that:

- Half of all households headed by workers ages 55-64 have less than $88,000 in retirement accounts.

- 71% of Americans between the ages of 45 and 64 admit they are worried about having enough money for retirement.

- The average family with at least one credit card has over $10,000 in credit card debt.

Between my personal experience following the status quo and the overwhelming preponderance of evidence, we know the status quo isn't working. We can also look at advocates of conventional wisdom to see what they are doing to determine if it's a good idea.

Suzy Ormond, a widely known financial advice giver, estimates her net worth at $25 million dollars. You can find her on TV and in books recommending that her audience invest in mutual funds as the foundation for their savings. Based on the advice she gives, I would assume she has the majority of her savings in mutual funds if for no other reason than a little self-dignity.

So, it came to many as a surprise when asked about where the majority of her money is invested. Outside of her $7 million in real estate, she said, "I buy zero coupon municipal bonds; and all the bonds I buy are AAA rated and insured, so even if the city goes under I get my money." When asked about the stock market Ormond said, "I have a million dollars in the stock market because if I lose a million dollars I don't personally care."

Hmmm. That may be a little of "Do what I say, not what I do."

It should be noted that Ormond's show appears on CNBC, a TV station that has A LOT of ad revenue from big Wall Street firms. Also, TD Ameritrade is a sponsor of Ormond, and they make significant revenue from facilitating stock and mutual fund trades.

Ormond certainly has no monopoly among financial gurus whose advice can cost you; but for the sake of brevity, we will only use her as an example to illustrate some of the conflicts that exist.

2. Financial Success Without the Rollercoaster

    "Do you wish to rise? Begin by descending. You plan a tower that will pierce the clouds? Lay first the foundation." –Saint Augustine

    There is good news…you can be financially successful without the rollercoaster ride of the market.

Your long-term financial success is more dependent on the foundation you lay than the total rate of return you achieve (or, in many cases, the rate of return you hope to achieve, but do not). This is not emphasized among the pop culture gurus for any number of reasons, but I suspect a couple of them are:

- *Talking about a solid foundation is not nearly as sexy and exciting as talking about chasing rates of return.* Think about your dream house. You most likely get excited about the kitchen, or the master bedroom or the basement but not about the foundation that it is all built on. Yet, we know intuitively that dream rooms won't exist for long without a solid foundation. The same is true financially.

- *The institutions in America have little incentive for you to be aware of the need for a solid foundation.* Banks make higher profits with high balances on credit cards and loans. Wall Street has more profits with more money and more transactions chasing rates of returns. Governments benefit from your spending... sales tax revenue, tax revenue on the profits from stores and vendors, and in the long run, you have to delay retirement, so there are more years to tax your income.

Your personal financial house needs to be built to withstand the storms known as *unexpected life events.* Just like your regional location determines the likelihood of various storms (hurricanes, tornadoes, earthquakes, tsunamis, typhoons, floods, droughts, etc.) your stage of life also has various storms and life events that can threaten your financial success (job loss, decrease in income, illness, disability, premature death, living longer than expected, lawsuits, tax changes, health care expenses, care of a loved one like a child or parent, etc).

If your plan does not include safe money strategies and products built on a solid foundation to withstand *life events*, all the while achieving good rates of return, then it's a plan built for failure. Because safe money tools and strategies that should be used, vary in each unique situation, I will not go into them now; but you need to know, they are available to be utilized even though the rest of the world may not want you to know.

When developing a plan utilizing safe money strategies as the foundation for success, you should look at your ultimate goal. For example, look at a **worry free** retirement income of $35,000 a year, and then look at the strategies to achieve that goal with as little risk as possible. Lower risk means higher likelihood of achieving the goal. Your goal should not be built around a casino crapshoot or with a hope and a prayer that things work out.

3. Successful Investing in the Market

It is possible to be successful investing in the stock market after building on a safe money foundation, if you are built emotionally for the ups and downs. But it is not done the way Wall Street and financial gurus would have you do it.

Two of the more typical myths put out by the Wall Street and the general media are that there is a person or group of people who can consistently and predictably be successful timing the market, based on economic forecasts and there are Wall Street experts who can consistently pick the best stocks.

To debunk the approach of timing the market based on forecasts, I only need a quote from former Federal Reserve Chairman Alan Greenspan, "The Fact that our economical models at The Fed, the best in the world, have been wrong for fourteen straight quarters, does not mean they will not be right in the fifteenth quarter."

Staying with the use of quotes from experts to act as

myth busters, I share with you quotes from two touted stock pickers just prior to the 2008 melt down:

AIG "could have huge gains in the second quarter." – Bijan Moazami, analyst, Friedman, Billings, Ramsey, May 9, 2008.) AIG lost $5 billion that quarter and $25 billion the following quarter and eventually was taken over by the government.

"I think Bob Steel's the one guy I trust to turn this bank around, which is why I've told you on weakness to buy Wachovia." – Jim Cramer, *CNBC commentator, Mar. 11, 2008.* Two weeks later, Wachovia came within hours of failure as depositors fled. Steel eventually agreed to a takeover by Wells Fargo. Wachovia shares lost half their value from September 15 to December 29.

So, we know timing the market and stock picking don't work. What do we need to do be successful investing the market?

For starters, we need a really long-time horizon (like 20 years) and emotional stability to avoid fear and panic. If you don't have these two things taken care of, you need to revisit where your money is invested.

Then, you need to get an analysis to find out nine things about your money invested in the market:

- What is the specific statistic measure of risk within my portfolio?

- How diversified am I really, or do I just own a lot of stuff?

- Historically, based on my risk and asset classes

owned, what is my potential for loss in a market crash and will I be ok when it happens again?

- How much overlap is there within my portfolio? (Do I have different mutual funds owning the same thing?)

- Over the long run, what is my expected rate of return?

- An efficiency evaluation to determine if you're maximizing you rate of return for the amount of risk you have taken on

- Is my advisor acting as a fiduciary on my ccount?

- How is the 3-factor model of investing being applied to my portfolio?

- What are the average transactions with my portfolio? (Transactions can drive costs higher and returns lower.)

Because advisors and brokers are traditionally Wall Street trained, they aren't always informed on how to get this information. If you are going to be in the market, be certain these items are addressed so you are maximizing your dollars for your benefit and not Wall Street's benefit

On the way to your dreams…

We use the term "retire rich" not in hopes of inspiring greed or promising the doubling of money overnight; but because we believe if you build a foundation using the ideas and strategies shared with you, that you can ultimately remove the emotional fear and anxiety that prevents us from maximizing the difference we can make within our families, communities, or whatever you may hold dear. In our opinion, this is "retiring rich." We hope to change the way Americans save and invest their money in order to have more and more people retiring rich.

ABOUT EDDIE

Investment expert and entrepreneur, Eddie Overdyke, AIF, makes a science of investment products, making him one of the most knowledgeable and effective financial advisors in the country. Overdyke is the owner of Overdyke Wealth Advisory of Atlanta, Georgia. With a degree in Business Administration with a concentration in Finance, he is also an Accredited Investment Fiduciary® and a Qualified Safe Money Millionaire™ Advisor. He is established as a leader in his field and has been recognized in *The Atlanta Journal-Constitution* as well as nationally in *America's Top Hometown Financial Advisors*.

Overdyke is a retirement planning expert who works with individuals to assist them in strategic planning for a stable lifestyle after their working years. His company is structured as an independent firm to avoid any conflicts of interest and to act as an unbiased advocate for his clients. He is interested in creating long-term relationships and works from a standpoint of retirement success rather than from rates of return. He has been thoroughly trained on functional alternatives to Wall Street and has access to products that create a secure and guaranteed investment portfolio for his retirement clients. Realizing each client's situation to be unique, he thoroughly examines their individual needs, their risk tolerance, and their objectives to determine the appropriate investment vehicles.

Part of Overdyke's work is with small businesses in regard to employee retirement benefits and investment vehicles. He often works in conjunction with an employee benefits firm assisting them by handling the retirement plan options in the employer's benefit package. He is able to show employers how to uniquely structure a program for their employees to reduce the employer's costs and fees. He also educates employees on how they can most successfully utilize the retirement plan in which they invest.

Overdyke has recently been featured in *USA Today* as one of "America's Game Changers" in his industry. He also was the featured guest on the television program "Leading Experts" in Orlando, Florida. Additionally, he anticipates the release of his first book later this year. The book will address successful strategies on how to accumulate money, as well as, looking at Wall Street methodology and how it influences the psychology of personal investing.

Overdyke has also been asked to co-author an upcoming book entitled, *Out Front*. The book is a collection of writings by key leaders in various industries. According to the publisher's marketing personnel, both books are anticipated to quickly reach the bestseller list. Other initiatives planned by Overdyke this year include the launching of a radio program in the greater Atlanta area. Additional information about Overdyke and the services provided by Overdyke Wealth Advisory are available at the firm's website, www.overdykewa.com or by calling his office at 678-935-0952.

CHAPTER 15

5 WAYS TO DOUBLE YOUR BUSINESS USING ONLINE MARKETING

BY SHASHANK SHEKHAR

As a business owner do I really need to implement online marketing to grow my business? As an author, national speaker and online marketing consultant, I get this question asked a lot.

Depending on which research you follow, 70% to 92% of local consumers search online to find a business. Marketing

171

online isn't an option anymore – it's a requirement. That's where your prospects and customers are searching for businesses they can trust to buy from. Marketing Online is not just about having a website (even if you have a really good one). It's about being found where your customers are and engaging them on their turf. So, the bad news is you may have lost a ton of customers because you were not found when they were looking online. However, the good news is – only 26% of small businesses have invested any substantial time, or money to build a strong online presence. It's not too late to get started; the question is how? If you follow the 5 ways discussed later in this chapter, by the end of it, you will have an answer.

Start with a Strategy – Decide what you want to achieve. How much resources you are willing to commit? If you don't know what goal you are going after, how would you know if your online marketing plan has succeeded? In some cases, it could be fairly basic (and most important) goal of getting more leads/prospects. In other cases, you can go after an indirect goal that can result into leads/prospects at a later date. Some of those goals could be:

- Build a bigger database
- Get more likes/followers
- Manage your reputation online
- Build a bigger brand

Search Engine Optimization – The ultimate goal of a business online presence typically is to get on page 1 of Google search results. In my experience of helping several clients get there – it has been the biggest game-changer. If you are not on page 1 – you are practically invisible. Research suggests that 68% of searchers do not go beyond page 1 when searching for a keyword and 85% of them do not go beyond page 2. But even before we head into how you can optimize your website for better search engine results, let's talk about keywords.

Keyword Research:

Keyword research is one of the most important, but often ignored part of search engine optimization (SEO). A keyword (or key phrase) is any word/phrase that people search for. Before you go about working on your site, you need to figure out what do you want to rank for. Are enough people even searching for that?

Google's free adwords tool can help you do that. This free tool tells you how many people are searching for a certain keyword on a monthly basis. It can be found at – https://adwords.google.com/select/KeywordToolExternal. There are also paid tools like Data Tracker and Market Samurai.

There are 2 important things that Google looks at to decide which websites to rank higher – Relevance and Authority. Relevance is about how similar is the content of your website in relation to the keyword being searched, e.g. if someone is searching for a Dentist in Chicago and your website is all about that, then you are very relevant to Google. Authority is about how credible your site is. Let's see how we can build relevance and authority.

Building Relevance:

- Keyword match in the title of the website
- Keyword match in the description of the website
- Keyword match in the domain of the website

For example, if you are a real estate agent and want your website to rank for the keyword "New York Real Estate," it may be a good idea to get a domain name with both New York and Real Estate as part of the name. Title of the website could be – New York Real Estate, New York Homes for Sale and the description of the website could be –Get all the news about New York Real Estate, Get community information and Search all New York Homes for sale. Did you notice how the domain name, title of the website and description of the website all had "New York Real Estate" as a part of it – the same keyword you wanted to rank for?

Building Authority:

Write original and relevant content regularly – Adding more content to your website on a regular basis builds the credibility of your website quickly. A great way to do this is by blogging. In fact HubSpot reports that a company that blogs gets 55% more website visitors than a company that does not.

Build/get Inbound Link – Inbound links is the most important component of getting ranked higher in search results. However, be aware of the so-called inexpensive SEO companies that will build spammy links by paying for it to third party websites. These links used to work in the past, but with recent updates to Google algorithm, they can actually hurt your rankings. So stay away from that. There are some genuine and "white-hat" ways to get inbound links. Let's look at some:

Blogging – Not to keep harping on the benefits of blogging, but HubSpot did report that companies that blog get 97% more inbound links than the ones who do not. And don't just stop at blogging on your own sites – go a step further and guest blog on other relevant sites. It's a win-win for both parties – they get new content that would benefit their readers and you get a new audience and links back to your site. One such website where you can find guest blogging opportunities is www.MyBlogGuest.com

Easy Link Building Opportunities – Sometimes some of the most powerful link building opportunities are the ones that get overlooked the most. Some of them could be from your Chamber of Commerce website, from the website of a charitable cause you donate to, websites of your business/referral partners, website of industry association you are a member of, industry directory websites and the list goes on. The important part is to always be actively looking for inbound links and when you find an opportunity – don't let it slip.

Be present at other places – Being present at other places like Social Media Platforms and relevant online directories (mentioned later in this chapter) also contribute towards better search results.

Social Media Marketing- While SEO and other online/offline tools can be a great way to acquire clients, Social Media plays an important role in keeping them. There has never been a more effective yet very inexpensive way of owning your database and remaining on top of their mind.

Some of the top social media platforms today are: Facebook, Twitter, LinkedIn, Pinterest, Google Plus and FourSquare. Pick your platforms wisely because it may be difficult to manage too many of them. I advise my clients to pick two (tops three) platforms where they can be active, be able to engage with their audience and get the maximum value out of it. If you are a retail location that thrives on impulse purchase – Foursquare could be a good platform. If you are a company targeting professionals, LinkedIn will be a better idea. And if you sell something that has a lot of visual appeal like bridal dresses, Pinterest is your best bet. But almost in every case, Facebook is a must because of the sheer size of their active members and the time spent by those members on Facebook.

Here are some tips to get you started and get the maximum results from Facebook –

1. Start your own Business Page. It's free and easy. Start here and follow the prompts – http://www.facebook.com/pages/create.php

2. Once you have created the page make sure it looks good by choosing an attractive cover image and thumbnail.

3. Post useful content that will benefit and engage your audience. It could be a mix of news, events, discounts, coupons, polls, trivia, photos, videos etc.

4. Invite your clients and personal Facebook friends to "like" your page.

5. Rinse and repeat #3 and #4.

Local Online Directories – One of the easiest ways for a local business to become ubiquitous online, get found more often, and jump to page 1 of search results like Google and Bing is to be present on top online directories. There are several directories that you need to be present on. The two most important are:

Google Places – Google has already created millions of

pages for local businesses around the country. All you need is to go to http://www.google.com/places/ and claim your business listing. If your business is not listed there, you can create a new account. Claiming or creating a business listing will help you include more details, pictures, videos, specialties, coupons etc., making it more likely for visitors to your Google Places page to contact you. Google almost always has 5-7 Places listings on page 1 of search results when someone searches for a local business. So, your chances of getting there is extremely high with a highly optimized account. And did I mention – all this is free?

Yelp – It's the largest consumer review site in the country and is trusted by millions of web surfers. The majority of people searching for local businesses with social proof visit Yelp to read its reviews. You can create a free account or claim an existing business listing at https://biz.yelp.com/.

Some other directories that you should create your profile on are:

- YP.com
- Superpages
- City Merchant
- Insider Pages
- Manta
- Kudzu
- Yahoo Local
- Bing Local
- Merchant Circle
- Matchpoint
- Localeze
- InfoUSA

Interestingly, the more online directories that show your Business Name, Address and Phone Number (called NAP in short), the better your chances of ranking higher on Google Places listings.

Video Marketing – 53.5% of the population (~170 million) and 70.8% of Internet users (up 7.1% from 2011) will watch online video in 2012. And every year, from here on, will see increased video viewing online. Even with such high level of video consumption, businesses have been slow at creating videos. Whatever business you are in, there are various kinds of videos that you can create:

- Promote Your Business
- FAQs for Customers
- Client Testimonials
- Community Video
- Videos to remain in touch with your clients

There are several ways to produce such videos:

Screencasting – A screencast is a digital recording of computer screen output, also known as a video screen capture, often containing audio narration. If you are camera shy, this is a great way to get started with video creation since the viewer only gets to see what is on your screen and not you. This also works great for videos, which have lots of technical information. Some software you can use for screencasting is Camtasia (for PC and Mac) and Screenflow (for Mac only). Both of these are paid software with a free trial download available. You can also download completely free software called Jing from http://www.techsmith.com/download/jing/. Jing works with both Windows and Mac.

Using your video camera – The most common way of creating videos is by recording with your video camera. These days it's very easy to record HD quality videos using inexpensive cameras like Flip or Kodak Touch. And there is always your smart phone video camera, which just keeps getting better by day. Most of these videos need to be edited and computers these days ship with in-built video editing software like Movie Maker (for Windows) and iMovie (for Mac). You can get fancy and try software like Adobe Premiere, Final Cut Pro or Sony Vegas. But for most of your video editing needs the inbuilt software should be good enough. If you find learning some of the software challenging, use the tutorial videos or go to http://www.lynda.com/ (a fairly inexpensive way to learn a lot of software).

Using pre-made templates – This is probably the easiest way to crank out a professional grade video very quickly. One of my favorites is www.Animoto.com – it does exactly what their website says – "Turn your photos, video clips, and music into stunning video masterpieces to share with everyone." Give it a shot – you will be surprised how easy and fun video creation could be.

Distribution – Creating any kind of content is only half the job done. Getting those content found is the other half. Make sure you share your videos everywhere you can, starting with the biggest show in town – YouTube. Other places you can share your videos are Social Media Platforms you are present on, your own website/blog and other video sharing sites like Vimeo, Viddler, Metacafe etc.

WHAT'S NEXT?

Measure – Most marketers know the saying from John Wanamaker, considered the father of both the modern department store and modern advertising that goes: "I know that half of my advertising dollars are wasted ... I just don't know which half." So, it's important to constantly track and measure your results. If anything is not working, tweak it, change it or drop it altogether. If something *is* working, do more of it. Remember what Peter Drucker said: "What gets measured.... gets done."

Be patient – Depending on the strength of your online competition and the effort you put in, it could take a few months before you start seeing the results. But if you are patient and follow the 5 ways mentioned in this chapter diligently, in few short months you would have built a stellar online presence and attracted hundreds of new customers. This is the marketing channel of now and the future – invest appropriate amounts of time, effort and money into it.

Hire a Consultant – As a business owner myself, I understand it's not easy to wear so many hats. Some of the techniques talked about in this chapter may have a steep learning curve if it's an unknown territory for you. You may not have time and/or inclination to learn it on your own. Or even if you learn, it may not be the best use of your time to actively manage your online marketing. Instead of not getting it done at all because of lack of time – outsource to a consultant. Understand that the consultant also needs to understand your business systems and processes. Online marketing doesn't work in isolation; it has to be an integrated part of your entire business process. So preferably work with someone who has a business degree and/or has run their own business and have been successful with implementing online marketing for their business.

Bonus offer – Get a 30 minute free consulting session with me valued at $250 by completing the form at http://www.take2consulting.com/request-a-free-quote/. Mention, "OUTFRONT" in the subject line.

ABOUT SHASHANK

Shashank Shekhar is a published author, national speaker, online marketing expert and blogger. He has trained thousands of business owners on how to use online marketing tools to grow their business. He has been interviewed on several TV and radio shows and has been featured on various online outlets like Yahoo News, ABC and CBS News.

Shashank combines the power of online platforms and his business education background to help business owners find new client opportunities that they didn't even know existed. His proven techniques have helped business owners grow their business dramatically. What sets his ideas apart is that they are tried and tested. He started a lending company in 2008 with a zero database and produced close to $100 million in less than four years. He achieved this by using the same marketing and branding techniques that his clients have access to.

Shashank holds an MBA in marketing, and has worked for Fortune 500 companies like GE in managerial positions. He is currently the CEO of Take2 Consulting, a company that helps business owners grow their businesses using online marketing channels.

To know more about Shashank and to request a free 30-minute consulting session, go to www.Take2Consulting.com

CHAPTER 16

7 FIGURE WEBINAR AND TELESEMINAR SECRETS:

HOW TO MOTIVATE SIGN-UPS AND SALES

BY JW DICKS, NICK NANTON AND LINDSAY DICKS

While teleseminars and webinars are slightly different (the teleseminar is given over the telephone while the webinar is most frequently accessed via computer or tablet), the concept is the same. For the purposes of this chapter, we'll refer to both as *webinars* because it's shorter... and we don't have to type as many letters (hey, we're busy people, every little thing helps!).

No question, webinars are awesome selling tools for entrepreneurs, professionals or any small business. Whether you're a dentist who needs to explain a cosmetic dentistry procedure in more detail or a life coach promoting his or her mentoring program, webinars bring you the following advantages:

- **THEY BUILD TRUST AND CREDIBILITY.**

When you're talking about your field at length, your target market gets to see just how knowledgeable and skilled you are. That, in turn, makes them more likely to buy from you.

- **THEY GROW YOUR DATABASE.**

A free webinar instantly attracts people interested in what you're selling and enables you to expand your lead list; you're able to gather names and contact info that you might not be able to obtain otherwise.

- **THEY ENABLE RELATIONSHIPS.**

Your personality comes through and people get to connect with you on a more human level. As a result, they get more comfortable with you.

- **THEY ADD VALUE.**

Your regular customers are able to access, at no additional cost, whatever new information you're sharing. That makes them feel they're getting more bang for their buck.

- **THEY JUMPSTART SALES CONVERSIONS.**

For most of you, this is the biggest reward a teleseminar

or webinar can deliver; by educating the audience about a product or service, you feed their preexisting interest (if they weren't interested, they wouldn't be watching in the first place) and you can close the final sale more easily.

But you can't realize any of those huge advantages unless *you get an audience to participate.* In this chapter, we're going to share some of our secrets of promoting webinars to realize the maximum benefit from them – even after they're over!

Every year, we've been lucky enough to realize seven figure incomes from these tools. Now, we'd like to see you experience your own share of this phenomenal success. So, read on as we reveal proven techniques to unleash *your* webinar's moneymaking power!

PREPARING THE WEBINAR LAUNCH

First of all, you want to think about when you are going to schedule your webinar. For us, we've found that Tuesday afternoon at 2 p.m. is an ideal time – and then we will usually set up an *encore* of the webinar Thursday at 2. The encore is important, because we're dealing with a lot of busy people who might miss the initial webinar, but still want to participate (believe it or not, we once had a guy call us on his way back from a funeral who wanted to make sure he could still get access to it).

Now, we don't start promoting the webinar too far in advance of when it actually happens. We generally don't let people know about a Tuesday webinar until the Thursday before – that's just what works for us. The basic message, which we usually send out by e-mail, goes like this...

There's an amazing opportunity coming up next week, we'll give you all the details then, but you'd better sign up now for a spot.

At the end of the e-mail, we, of course, provide a link to our webinar sign-up page.

Now, that message is structured with the following two crucial ingredients:

- We don't provide too much detail, promoting it more as a "can't-miss" event. Too much detail will cause people to either say yes" or "no" right away. This way, they get more engaged in the process.

- We create scarcity to get them to sign up for the webinar ASAP. That's a call to action to get them to commit *now* – before they even really know what it's all about. And, since there's no cost for the webinar, it's not that hard of a commitment.

We then wait on sending the second e-mail out until Monday – the day before the webinar. Sending stuff out on Friday is usually a bad idea, because most people are either busy finishing up the week or are cutting out early for the weekend. Either way, they're preoccupied. One important part of your thought process must always be that your webinar is not everyone else's priority, and you need to make it as easy for *them* as possible.

When Monday comes around, however, we send out our second e-mail with an exciting attention-getting headline, such as: "Are you ready to become a best-selling author?" if we're going to unveil our latest book project. Inside the e-mail, we'll detail the value that book can bring to your marketing efforts, give details on the time of the webinar and, of course, embed a bunch of links where they can register for the webinar.

Finally, the day of the webinar, a third email goes out, basically saying: "It's TODAY. You shouldn't miss this." And again, we detail all the benefits and let them know that there's limited space available for this presentation.

EXTRA-ADDED PROMOTION

Now, we do webinars pretty regularly, and we have a system down. You may not do them as often – or you may have an extra special webinar that you want to make sure attracts the attention (and the sign-ups) it deserves. So, you might want to go above and beyond e-mail promotion to other avenues.

For instance, people actually still have fax machines – so you can do what's called a "Fax Blast" on the day of the webinar and simultaneously fax a reminder to all your clients at once. We find that the old technology makes a brand new impact simply because hardly anyone is using it anymore! There are various services out there that will help you accomplish this cheaply and easily without much hassle. Below is an example of a "Fax Blast" that my friend Nate Hagerty did for our joint teleseminar:

And speaking of old ways to send messages, you can also use the good ol' U.S. Postal System to get the job done. Below, you'll find another example from Nate – a postcard campaign promoting the same webinar:

Postcards are VERY cheap to send out and very effective (especially over-sized ones).

PUTTING SIZZLE IN YOUR SIGN-UP

Now, obviously, the website link has to take your prospects to a landing page that is going to clinch a sign-up. We find the best first step to making that happen is using *video*.

Some people think reading is too much work, but will happily click on a video to see what somebody has to say. Besides, if you're the person featured in the video, you have a chance to talk *directly* to the visitor and make your case as to why they should check out your webinar. As we say time and time again, people buy *people* – and video is the best online method to replicate one-on-one communication in the most powerful way.

Now, remember, it doesn't have to be *you* in the video. When we did a webinar about one of our Brian Tracy book projects, we didn't put ourselves in the landing page video – we put up a Brian Tracy video testimonial. Whoever the biggest name is that you can land, and whoever has the most credibility and best reputation, that's the person you want to in your video – because that's the person the visitor will be most likely to listen to and by swayed by.

Just because video might be the strongest arrow in your quiver, however, doesn't mean you should neglect the sales copy on your sign-up sheet. If you're thinking you can just slap on a simple webinar registration form under your video, you're letting go of the last chance you have to make sure of a sign-up.

It's important to reiterate the benefit that the webinar delivers, simply and strongly, on that landing page. Your prospect may have clicked on your e-mail link and gotten distracted.

A few minutes later, he or she may return to the computer and, in the meantime, have forgotten completely why your landing page is up on their computer. If you have the right copy on the screen to immediately remind them why they went there in the first place, you won't lose them.

That means you reintroduce yourself with your picture and credentials, and you give them bullet points on what value your webinar is going to add to the viewer's life. It's important to re-explain as much as possible, because maybe the person coming to your landing page didn't get your set-up e-mail blasts – maybe a friend forwarded the landing page link and just told the person to check it out.

For the actual opt-in, you want to get at least their first and last name and their e-mail address. You want to be able to address them by name when you send e-mails (and you obviously can't remind them about the webinar without the e-mail address!).

But something else you might want to go for is getting people's cell phone numbers, because there are systems that allow you to text-message reminders. These are much more effective that e-mail reminders and follow-ups, because, again, it's more of a one-on-one communication.

Many of us have thousands of e-mails in our inbox and a reminder can be easily lost in the herd; our personal experience is that a text reminder is much more effective at getting people on the phone or computer for your webinar. When you text ten minutes before you're about to start, it gives the event an extra sense of importance and urgency.

FROM WEBINAR TO SELLING TOOL

Now, let's face facts. Much as we think everyone in the world is dying to be a part of one of our webinars, there is a significant segment of quality leads out there that just won't do it. Which means, you've just made that tremendous effort; and, as far as that market segment goes, you've realized zero revenue.

Well, of course, you don't have to stand for that!

What we do is take the audio from the webinar, strip off the video if there is video, and burn it onto CDs for direct mailings. We don't like to do DVDs because many people will listen to a CD in the car, given the opportunity. Of course, we certainly don't want them watching DVDs while they drive. As two of us are lawyers, we understand the dangers of personal injury cases!

We also make sure to package the CD in a colorful and interesting way. Take a look at how we packaged the CD in the picture on the following page (and this is just an example, Jack and Nick really don't sell CDs to Lindsay, because she already knows what's on them...)

Many companies can take your handwriting and turn it into a font – as they did with Nick's in this instance. We also purposely picked paper to put the message on that was the color of the traditional Post-It – canary yellow. This mailing was designed for people who may have signed up and didn't participate. They've already signaled their interest; and, for whatever reason, they didn't show up for the event. Well, this CD is another chance to bring that webinar content right to their mailbox. We let them know it in the message; and, of course, we make sure to put their first name right on the note.

Now, for those on our list who didn't sign up for the webinar, we package the CD with a more detailed sales letter utilizing the same techniques. If you take a look at the picture below, you'll see an example of how we use the same *personal touch* to sell the benefits of the CD content to people who may be unfamiliar with what the webinar was all about. In this case, we used actual paper from legal pads and again used hand-writing font for the actual content of the sales letter.

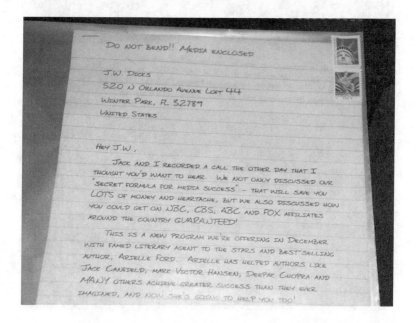

One thing I want you to notice is this particular package is hand-stamped. On this mailing, we didn't use a bulk meter rate. Why? Well, this technique confirms someone human actually put this package together, which means it doesn't appear to be traditional "junk mail." It has a far better chance of being opened that way. And, by the way, another little secret – get the biggest, nastiest, most ugly stamps you can find for this kind of direct mail campaign.

On the flip side pictured on the following page, you'll see how we designed the CD to spotlight Michael Gerber, the big name associated with this particular project – another attention-getter to those who might know Michael more than they might know us (hard as that is to believe, LOL).

One final trick I'd like to share with you: another great way to get more bang for your webinar buck is to get a transcription of the audio from the webinar and have it transformed into a *sales letter*. All your sales points are right there, and it can really take down your copywriting costs – often an expensive undertaking.

The limited space of this chapter prevents us from sharing all our webinar money making secrets; but, be aware, there is a *lot* more to share, such as how to craft a compelling offer, how to create price points that boost sales, and so forth.

But we will actually give you *one last secret* of how we get the most from our webinars – this chapter has been based on a transcript from a webinar about this very subject!

We invite you to contact us if you'd like to know more about our 7 Figure Webinar Secrets. And, as always, we wish you good luck with all your entrepreneurial endeavors!

ABOUT JW

JW Dicks, Esq., is America's foremost authority on using personal branding for business development. He has created some of the most successful brand and marketing campaigns for business and professional clients to make them the Credible Celebrity Expert in their field and build multi-million-dollar businesses using their recognized status.

JW Dicks has started, bought, built, and sold a large number of businesses over his 39-year career and developed a loyal international following as a business attorney, author, speaker, consultant, and business expert's coach. He not only practices what he preaches by using his strategies to build his own businesses, he also applies those same concepts to help clients grow their business or professional practice the way he does.

JW has been extensively quoted in such national media as *USA Today, Wall Street Journal, Newsweek, Inc.* magazine, Forbes.com, CNBC.com, and Fortune *Small business*. His television appearances include ABC, NBC, CBS and FOX affiliate stations around the country. He is the resident branding expert for Fast Company's internationally syndicated blog and is the publisher of Celebrity Expert Insider, a monthly newsletter targeting business- and brand-building strategies.

JW has written over 22 books, including numerous best-sellers, and has been inducted into the National Academy of Best Selling Authors. JW is married to Linda, his wife of 39 years, and they have two daughters, two granddaughters and two Yorkies. JW is a 6th generation Floridian and splits time between his home in Orlando and his beach house on the Florida west coast.

ABOUT NICK

An Emmy Award-Winning Director and Producer, Nick Nanton, Esq., is known as the Top Agent to Celebrity Experts around the world for his role in developing and marketing business and professional experts, through personal branding, media, marketing and PR to help them gain credibility and recognition for their accomplishments. Nick is recognized as the nation's leading expert on personal branding as *Fast Company* magazine's Expert Blogger on the subject and lectures regularly on the topic at at major universities around the world. His book *Celebrity Branding You®* has also been used as the textbook on personal branding for University students.

The CEO of The Dicks + Nanton Celebrity Branding Agency, an international agency with more than 1,000 clients in 26 countries, Nick is an award-winning director, producer and songwriter who has worked on everything from large scale events to television shows with the likes of Bill Cosby, President George H.W. Bush, Brian Tracy, Michael Gerber and many more.

Nick is recognized as one of the top thought-leaders in the business world and has co-authored 16 best-selling books alongside Brian Tracy, Jack Canfield (creator of the *Chicken Soup for the Soul* Series), Dan Kennedy, Robert Allen, Dr. Ivan Misner (Founder of BNI), Jay Conrad Levinson (Author of the *Guerilla Marketing* Series), Leigh Steinberg and many others, including the breakthrough hit *Celebrity Branding You!*®

Nick has published books by Brian Tracy, Mari Smith, Jack Canfield, Dan Kennedy and many other celebrity experts, and Nick has led the marketing and PR campaigns that have driven more than 600 authors to Best-Seller status. Nick has been seen in *USA Today*, *Wall Street Journal*, *Newsweek*, *Inc.* magazine, *The New York Times*, *Entrepreneur®* magazine and, FastCompany.com, and has appeared on ABC, NBC, CBS, and FOX television affiliates around the country, as well as CNN, FOX News, CNBC, and MSNBC from coast to coast, speaking on subjects ranging from branding, marketing and law to American Idol.

Nick is a member of the Florida Bar, holds a JD from the University of Florida Levin College of Law, as well as a BSBA in Finance from the University of Florida's Warrington College of Business. Nick is a voting member of The National Academy of Recording Arts & Sciences (NARAS, Home to The GRAMMYs), a member of The National Academy of Television Arts & Sciences (Home to the Emmy Awards), co-founder of the National Academy of Best-Selling Authors, an 11-time Telly Award winner, and spends his spare time working with Young Life and Downtown Credo Orlando and rooting for the Florida Gators with his wife, Kristina, and their three children, Brock, Bowen and Addison.

ABOUT LINDSAY

Lindsay Dicks helps her clients tell their stories in the online world. Being brought up around a family of marketers, but a product of Generation Y, Lindsay naturally gravitated to the new world of online marketing. Lindsay began freelance writing in 2000 and soon after launched her own PR firm that thrived by offering an in-your-face "Guaranteed PR" that was one of the first of its type in the nation.

Lindsay's new media career is centered on her philosophy that "people buy people." Her goal is to help her clients build a relationship with their prospects and customers. Once that relationship is built and they learn to trust them as the expert in their field, then they will do business with them. Lindsay also built a patent-pending process that utilizes social media marketing, content marketing and search engine optimization to create online "buzz" for her clients that helps them to convey their business and personal story. Lindsay's clientele span the entire business map and range from doctors and small business owners to Inc 500 CEOs.

Lindsay is a graduate of the University of Florida. She is the CEO of CelebritySites™, an online marketing company specializing in social media and online personal branding. Lindsay is also a multi-best-selling author including the best-selling book *Power Principles for Success,* which she co-authored with Brian Tracy. She was also selected as one of America's PremierExperts® and has been quoted in *Newsweek,* the *Wall Street Journal, USA Today,* and *Inc.* magazine as well as featured on NBC, ABC, and CBS television affiliates speaking on social media, search engine optimization and making more money online. Lindsay was also recently brought on FOX 35 News as their Online Marketing Expert.

Lindsay, a national speaker, has shared the stage with some of the top speakers in the world, such as Brian Tracy, Lee Milteer, Ron LeGrand, Arielle Ford, David Bullock, Brian Horn, Peter Shankman and many others. Lindsay was also a Producer on the Emmy-nominated film Jacob's Turn.

You can connect with Lindsay at:
Lindsay@CelebritySites.com
www.twitter.com/LindsayMDicks
www.facebook.com/LindsayDick

CHAPTER 17

SIMPLE ISN'T EASY, BUT IT WORKS:

5 SIMPLE STEPS TO BECOMING A SUCCESSFUL ONLINE ENTREPRENEUR

BY LAURA WAAGE

It was 2009 and I was leaving corporate America after 15-plus years of playing in the corporate sandbox. By society's measuring stick, I was a success in the business world; but personally, I wasn't happy. I felt trapped, caged and held hostage by the confines of a lifestyle that monetarily gave me everything I wanted; but personally left me starving for more.

I wanted more freedom, more flexibility. I wanted the fruits of my labors to serve a more meaningful purpose. I wanted to start living life on my terms and doing it in a way that allowed me to shine brightly while still being true to myself.

It's not that I didn't want to work hard – don't mistake me. I just didn't want to continue to do it for someone else, on his or her terms.

I had been in sales and marketing in the technologies field for over a decade, where I had a passionate love affair with technology. I was enamored by the ways in which online technologies were changing the landscape of our world. A major shift was occurring, and suddenly opportunities that were previously reserved for large corporations with big, lofty budgets were now available to the common person.

I realized this was *it*. I had found my calling. I wanted to be an online entrepreneur. But wait... what does that even mean?

I went through a discovery process spending thousands of hours and tens of thousands of dollars learning everything I could about becoming an online entrepreneur. And what I quickly realized was that many "online entrepreneurs" had a love of money, but not necessarily a love of their craft.

If I wanted it to be just about the money, I would've stayed in my previous field. What I wanted was passion. I wanted to love what I was doing and to bounce out of bed every day excited to *work*. I did not want to be another drone that complained day in and day out about my J-O-B. I wanted to let my energy, enthusiasm and passion shine.

As I contemplated my wants and challenged myself on whether or not this was a utopian dream, I was led to step one of what would evolve into my *5 Simple Steps for Becoming a Successful Online Entrepreneur.*

STEP 1 – DISCOVER YOUR PASSIONS

Money alone was not enough – it was not my motivating factor. I needed to discover my true passions. I took a step back and asked myself, "What do I lose myself in? How do hours pass by without me knowing that the sun has set? What would I do forever, even if I did it for free?"

I spent hours evaluating these questions and introspecting my discoveries. As I did, it became glaringly obvious. My three biggest passions are teaching, technology and Disney. But how could those three things possibly fit together in a way that could become the basis for my journey as an online entrepreneur? I didn't know the answer to this question *yet*... but I did share Walt Disney's belief that "All your dreams can come true if you have the courage to pursue them."

During this process of discovery, I also realized that many people go through their entire lives without ever discovering their true passions. Knowing what I now know, I wish this had been a class in high school – it would serve our future leaders better than another history class. But since it's not, I've put together some resources for discovering your passions, which can be found at www.LauraWaage.com/OutFront.

STEP 2 – FIND A MONETIZABLE NICHE

I was very fortunate to be able to interact with, and ask questions of, many successful online entrepreneurs. What I learned was that failure to properly research in advance of launching a project was one of the most common mistakes that many of them made. I'm no dummy. I chose to learn from *their* mistakes and made research a standard part of my process.

Turning my passions into online profits would only be effective if I identified a tightly targeted audience that had a want or a need for my passions. After all, I always think my own ideas are great, but if nobody else shares that same thought, then my business would go nowhere.

Doing proper research to identify this audience prior to launching is paramount to online success. And thanks to the Internet, performing this research is a fairly simple task.

The basic steps are:

I. **Find the Niche within your Niche.** Many people instinctively gravitate toward a market instead of a niche. The broader your topic, the harder it will be to find success. As an example, *Baseball Gear* is a market; *Left-Handed Baseball Gloves* is a targeted niche.

II. **Perform Keyword Research.** Keywords equal demand, therefore identifying the long-tail keywords that people are searching for will help you uncover a monetizable, targeted niche. There are several tools available to help you quickly and easily identify this information, including Google's Keyword Tool, Wordtracker and Market Samurai.

III. **Evaluate Market Competition.** If there is no competition for your product or service, there's a good chance that there is no market for it either. On the other hand, if there is too much competition, then the market may be overly saturated making it more difficult for you to find success. Finding the right balance is essential.

If you're struggling trying to identify a monetizable niche and would like access to the step-by-step research process that I follow, please visit www.LauraWaage.com/OutFront.

With clarity around my passions and my target market and niche identified, it was now time to move on to the next step.

STEP 3 – CREATE AN ACTION PLAN

Early on in my sales career I quickly learned that without an action plan, consistent success was hard to achieve. Sure, I would have the occasional win, which would have been fine if I had occasional bills, but that's not how life works.

Experience has taught me that without a detailed plan, a person will only spin their wheels and travel in circles. For this reason, exploring how to craft a detailed, action-oriented plan for the online entrepreneur became especially important to me.

Over the last two years, I have helped nearly 100 people on a one-on-one basis create plans for their online businesses. I evaluated what worked and what didn't, and studied the psychology behind why some people could stick to a plan when others could not.

The conclusion I came to was that first you have to know if the plan is for a left or right brained person, and then you have to design the plan to match their primary modality. A left-brained person tends to function best with a linear plan that is task oriented, while a right-brained person tends to function best with a visual plan that is goal oriented.

In both cases, the plan includes tasks, goals and objectives; but the layout and perception of that plan can have an overwhelming impact on a person's ability to succeed with it.

This was an eye opening revelation. It allowed me to put together a system for crafting action oriented plans that are designed to support someone's natural train of thought and propel them forward.

It also taught me the importance of building accountability into a plan. Whether it's with a coach, a business partner, or a professional colleague, having someone that reviews your plan and helps you to stay on track with it is essential.

The Online Entrepreneur's Action Plan is detailed and deliberate, covering many topics including:

- Online Business Model (Affiliate Marketing, Info Products, Physical Products, etc.)

- Type of Platform (Website, Blog, eCommerce Site, Fan Page, etc.)

- Technology (Wordpress, AutoResponder, Shopping Cart, Merchant Account, etc.)

- Content (Blog Posts, White Papers, Video Tutorials, etc.)

- Social Media Platforms (Pinterest, Facebook, Twitter, LinkedIn, etc.)

- Traffic Drivers (Paid Ads, Article Marketing, E-mail Marketing, SEO, etc.)

- Sales Funnel (Product Price Points, Multi-tiered Offers, etc.)

- Outsourcing (Website Development/Management, Content Creation, etc.)

- Customer Support (Helpdesk, Escalation Process, etc.)

- Offline Marketing Integration (Speaking Engagements, Direct Mail, etc.)

Benjamin Franklin once said: "By failing to prepare, you are preparing to fail." Sadly, I've seen way too many people fail simply because they didn't take the time to properly plan. I cannot stress the importance of this step enough.

If you're in the throes of creating an action plan and would like access to some valuable resources, please visit www.LauraWaage.com/OutFront.

STEP 4 – MEASURE, TEST AND TRACK

Not all things go according to plan, and some of the best-laid plans can fall short. So my strong advice (coming from a severe perfectionist who learned this lesson from experience) is to reward yourself for identifying areas that need improvement without punishing yourself for things that went awry. There's a reason for the saying "Hindsight is 20-20."

The other thing to always keep in mind is that the Internet is in a constant state of change and evolution. I recently read an article discussing the fact that technology has changed more in the last 15 years than it had from the beginning of time, up until 15 years ago. This is an astonishing fact, but one that online entrepreneurs experience the severity of on a daily basis. Don't believe me? Ask the Pandas and Penguins! (Geek humor, laugh with me)

When it comes to measuring, testing and tracking, you want to initiate this practice with every aspect of your online business. This includes your website or blog, your social media efforts, your e-mail marketing campaigns – all of it.

Tools have been developed to support every aspect, and many of them are free.

Two of my favorite resources for testing and tracking the success of websites are Google Analytics and www.StatMyWeb.com, which I use in conjunction with one another. Both are very easy to use and interpret and will provide you with valuable insights into what's working and what's not working within your site.

When it comes to measuring social media statistics, I use Hootsuite, but I also recommend SocialOomph. Both solutions offer great analytics packages and will empower you to maximize your social media efforts.

These are just a few examples of the testing and tracking solutions that are available; but if you'd like to see a more comprehensive list, please visit www.LauraWaage.com/OutFront.

STEP 5 – OPTIMIZE

The road to success is *not* a straight line. Just as a series of left and right turns are required for you to get from your home to the grocery store, there will be many turns required on your road to business success. The reality is you will encounter your fair share of speed bumps, red lights, flat tires and fender benders; but keep your eyes on the road ahead.

Steps 4 and 5 are a never-ending loop. They are also the guardrails on your business highway. Step 4 will point out the potholes, while Step 5 will put you back on a smooth road.

In any successful business – online or off – a constant cycle of *correct and continue* is required. If a business stays stagnant, it will die a slow and painful death. So, whether you need to make small tweaks or major shifts, use the results of your testing and tracking to continually steer your online business. Over time, the steering process becomes easier and ultimately leads to your growth and success.

Simple isn't easy, but it works. These 5 Simple Steps to Becoming a Successful Online Entrepreneur made my utopian dream a reality, and now it's your turn. Shine Bright!

ABOUT LAURA

Laura Waage is an author, speaker and online entrepreneur who spent more than a decade as a sales manager, consultant, trainer and presenter in technology fields. During that time, she worked with thousands of businesses of varying sizes, helping them to design better business practices, increase their revenues and create heightened customer experiences.

In 2009 Laura grew restless with the corporate America environment and leveraged her extensive business background to make the leap from employee to entrepreneur. Her background and love for technology led her straight to the world of Internet marketing, and she hasn't looked back since.

With a natural gift for teaching and training, Laura has traveled the globe helping others to identify their passions and to turn them into online profits. She lives by a life quote from Maya Angelou that says: "When you learn, teach. When you get, give."

Laura openly shares her knowledge and gifts in a quest to empower as many people as possible to be successful. For reading this book, she has prepared a special gift for you that can be claimed now by visiting www.LauraWaage.com/OutFront.

When not working, Laura enjoys spending time with her teenage daughter, traveling to foreign countries, and immersing herself in anything Disney.

You can connect with Laura at:

www.LauraWaage.com
contact@LauraWaage.com
www.twitter.com/Laura_Waage
www.facebook.com/LauraWaageOnline
www.pinterest.com/LauraWaage

CHAPTER 18

THRIVE-ONOMICS:

HOW TO DEPLOY THE 5 SECRET WEAPONS TO TRANSFORM YOUR BUSINESS FROM SURVIVING TO THRIVING!

BY SHANE AND LISA ADAMS

According to the Small Business Administration only 49% of small businesses survive past the five-year mark.

Think about it. Over half of those start-ups end up failing.

It stands to reason, then, that those entrepreneurs who succeed with their start-ups past that crucial five-year period deserve to be congratulated. They've beaten the odds and proven they have what it takes to be successful.

As business coaches, we've noticed these business owners share a lot of similarities. They launch a company in a specific industry in which they've already proven themselves. Their existing skills and influence serve as a catalyst to their success, by attracting to the company an array of loyal customers (often through word-of-mouth marketing that goes viral) as well as an ongoing stream of new prospects.

These entrepreneurs are, of course, happy with their initial financial successes – but they don't rest on their laurels. Instead, they look for opportunities to grow their businesses to the next level, so they can achieve even more. These *Next Level Entrepreneurs* begin to pursue these opportunities, not knowing that this next stage of business development may actually be even *more* challenging than the first five years.

Here's why. While increased sales and an expanding customer base are obviously good things, all that growth does have a downside. To put it simply, the bigger an operation becomes, the harder it is to keep up with all the growth.

Most entrepreneurs handle the challenges of growth by focusing on surface issues like putting out fires as they pop up, so they can keep up with increasing demand for their products and services. Unfortunately, they often fail to recognize and address the root causes of those fires – which means, things keep getting harder as growth continues.

It becomes a vicious cycle. More fires erupt – more effort,

energy and time is required to put them out, progress slows and systems begin to crack at the seams. Eventually, something *has* to give.

We call this the *Founder's Bottleneck Syndrome.*

Founder's Bottleneck Syndrome, or FBS, occurs when growth overwhelms a business, indicated by lower profitability and a higher degree of anxiety. The business owner may have trouble sleeping at night or start to see strains in their marriage and family life. At its worst, FBS can leave a successful business owner feeling like the strands of their life and business are unraveling. And while they may finally recognize that they need a plan to turn things around, they most likely have no idea what that plan should be.

That's where a business coach can make a world of difference. We ourselves have dealt with this situation time and time again; and that's why we've developed simple, proven ways to help this kind of entrepreneur not only to get a handle on where their business is now, but also to take it to the next level of success.

If you're afflicted with FBS, we're afraid there aren't any prescription drugs out there that can help – but our systems can. They've been designed to help you reach a position where:

- **Income can be grown at will,** by simply turning the sales funnel on.

- **You become the leader** in your marketplace.

- You build a loyal customer base, so every offer becomes the next **have-to-have purchase.**

- **Exclusivity** is created.

- Your business is **recession-proof.**

- You have a clear field with **no direct competitors.**

- Your business is **scalable, thriving and can fulfill the demands of sales.**

- Growing your business takes **less effort and is full of fun and excitement**

Maybe all this sounds like more of a dream business than any that could really exist, or maybe you think you have to die to have a company like this – by going to business heaven.

The good news is that no sleep or loss of life is required. What *is* required, however, is the correct strategic direction, as well as, ongoing consistency and disciplined action, to build your thriving and sustainable *dream* business. And the funny thing is, despite all the hard work entrepreneurs put into starting up their businesses, many are not willing to do what it takes to reach the next level.

Result? Those companies end up simply surviving, without experiencing the very rich rewards that could come from embracing what we call...

Thrive-onomics!

DEFINING THRIVE-ONOMICS:

Here's a disclaimer. Thrive-onomics isn't the most sexy and exciting approach in the world. But, hey, if we called it Consistency, Discipline and Focused Effort, would you have read this far? Probably not! Still, Thrive-onomics will cure you of your FBS and move you on to that next heavenly level of success.

A business that's destined to only survive tends to have a limited outlook. It's likely to be driven primarily by immediate sales, doesn't really have many long-term strategies in place, and has very few, if any, written operations. This type of business is heavily dependent on the competency of their employees – which means, when a key person moves on, it can spell disaster.

If you have a business like this, a business that's survived those crucial first few years, chances are you have a deep desire to take it further, to the point where you are financially independent. Chances are you're more than willing to put in the hard work necessary to get there. But chances are also good that you're also beginning to see that hard work alone is not enough. You know you need something more – but you don't know what that might be.

We do. In fact, we know from experience that there are five key *secret weapons* you need to deploy in order to conquer your current status quo and declare victory in achieving that next level of success.

Ready to hear how to thrive instead of merely survive? Then read on.

SECRET WEAPON #1 PLAN!

A successful business begins with having a viable vision in place; you must develop a clear strategic plan of what success looks like and the action steps it will take to get there.

That means identifying where your company is today, what results you're aiming to achieve, and what will need to be done differently in order to achieve those results.

That last step is where a lot of companies fall short. They often do a great job of articulating the results and the plan, but they fail to drill down deep enough to distinguish what specific behaviors and actions will create those results. So, they keep doing the same thing over and over, year after year, preoccupied by daily activities, just hoping they will reach their goals.

Simply defining your results and saying, "This is what I want," isn't enough. You have to also define the behaviors that will allow you to achieve those results – and create specific goals to encourage those behaviors.

You also need to put your plan in writing. Many business owners never take the time to actually write out their company's future – instead, they only talk about their dreams and what they want to achieve. Only by creating the right action steps – and committing to them in writing – will you actually connect where you are now to where you want to be.

You've no doubt heard of the gap between intentions and results. You can close that gap with a clear focus and a detailed plan of action.

SECRET WEAPON #2 SYSTEMIZE YOUR BUSINESS

If processes and systems aren't things you normally think about, the thought of deploying this secret weapon might sound a little overwhelming. However, they're not that hard to tackle.

Think of it this way: Each aspect of your business is made up of tasks: sales tasks, marketing tasks, accounting tasks, etc. When a group of tasks are linked together, they create a *process*. Those processes are then integrated into *systems*.

When you are able to identify all your processes and your systems, you gain a *Big Picture* perspective that is crucial to the successful management of your business. For example, let's look at your marketing systems – specifically, how you acquire new customers. By mapping out each process, you will get a clear picture of exactly how the overall system functions. The key is to come up with visual representations of each step, from the moment a prospect expresses interest, all the way to the delivery and follow up.

A map of your processes will show you where there are systemic gaps that need to be addressed and where there are redundancies that you can streamline. You'll see how each task relates to the next to create a process, and you can then assess the entire system to make sure it is aligned and working efficiently to create the best result possible.

Doing this for each process moves you that much closer to your company working as a total system, which frees you from having to rely on the competency and experience of any one individual. This makes employee transitions easier and a lot less of a hassle. It also allows you to see whether all processes are aligned with the overall goals and strategies of the business.

When the right systems have been refined and strategically placed, they become automatic; you're able to leverage your people and processes, which in turn, means you deliver a more consistent and predictable level of quality.

SECRET WEAPON #3 YOUR PEOPLE

Even the most effective systems can only take you so far – if you don't have the right staff in place. In fact, the best investment you can make in transforming your business is to develop your people into superstar employees.

The best and most natural place to start is at the top with you, the company's owners and your leadership team. It's essential to your company's overall plan that their actions and behaviors are consistent with your goals and line up with your messaging. And don't forget, it's also important that *your* attitudes and beliefs are in line with the company's strategies.

In other words, you need to walk your talk.

Much like parenting, leading a business effectively requires consistency and delivery of action. When you lead by example, you set the tone for everyone involved in your business from the top down.

We understand that this isn't always easy. Many companies start with an entrepreneur who has worked hard to master the technical aspect of the business. As the business grows, however, that entrepreneur needs to move away from that skill and into management; he or she needs to manage everyone else's role in the operations and processes of the company – areas where he or she might feel less comfortable.

However, these are skills and talents that can be developed and learned. Be open to new possibilities as you make this critical transition, and you'll find yourself becoming a more effective leader – and getting a stronger response from your people.

SECRET WEAPON #4 INTERNAL CUSTOMERS

Just like your customers, your employees have an essential relationship with your company. That's why we call your employees your *internal customers*. You need to work to build and develop the relationships with the same trust and credibility as you do with the people who patronize your business.

There is a direct link between how your internal customers feel about working for you and how they, in turn, interact with your company's customers. That's why you have to ask yourself the following questions:

- Do your employees believe in your company and what it stands for and delivers?

- Are they raving fans?

- How engaged are they in their work and what is their level of commitment?

- Are they an integral part of developing the company plan and process improvement?

- Do they possess the skills and knowledge necessary to accomplish their role in the plan?

- How developed are their attitudes and behaviors to provide the best experience for your external customers?

Your employees are usually the people who work most closely with your customers. They know the everyday systems and processes probably better than you, so they're usually the best source to consult when you want to improve them. If you want your internal customers to deliver the best to your external customers, then invest in them and give them all the resources necessary to do their jobs.

You'll find that *people power* can propel quantum shifts in your company.

SECRET WEAPON #5 "LOYAL CUSTOMERS = PROFITABILITY"

Customer loyalty is the linchpin of exponential profitability. Think of those companies that are famous for customer loyalty – household names that boast legions of loyal fans who just can't wait to buy their next product.

Disney. Apple. Google. What makes companies like those stand out from the pack? They specialize in creating *exceptional points of connection* with their customers.

The driving force behind most purchases – even when it's a large one such as a car or a house – is usually *emotional*. Experience is everything to a buyer. Unfortunately, so many businesses oversell and under-deliver that we're conditioned to be disappointed.

But that's why the companies we mentioned earlier stand out. That all-too-common disappointment others deliver is actually an opportunity for you to shine brighter than they do. The great brands are very clear about what their business is, and they have in place a unique and repeatable process for hiring, developing and training their employees to deliver an exceptional experience to each and every customer – every single time.

If you can do that in your business, whatever it may be...you, too, will experience Thrive-onomics!

Now, the five Secret Weapons we have discussed aren't really all *that* secret. As a matter of fact, they're already right there in your company's arsenal. When you use them as outlined in this chapter, they will enable you to create the kind of growing and thriving company that produces sustainable results in all economic environments.

However, just as an expedition to the top of Everest needs Sherpa guides with the know-how and expertise to get everyone safely to the top, you may need a business coach to help you objectively assess your current company's operation, as well as what's needed to help you reach the next level of success.

It's amazing to watch ordinary companies transform into extraordinary companies – with awesome results to match. Reaching a level of success that's sustainable, scalable and growing beyond your wildest dreams can be the biggest rush of all.

That's the power of Thrive-onomics.

We wish you all the best in your endeavors and please feel free to contact us at www.mythrivecoach.com for more information on this topic.

ABOUT SHANE AND LISA

Shane and Lisa Adams believe in the power of people – especially the power of dynamic entrepreneurs who are dedicated to small business success. For over twenty years, this husband-and-wife team has devoted themselves to mastering the intricacies of the small business world, experiencing it first-hand as owners, developers and strategic performance coaches. Along the way, they've learned exactly what it takes to launch a company, to prosper as a successful entrepreneur, and even to turn mom-and-pop start-ups into multi-million dollar enterprises.

Their passion is helping business owners realize dreams.

The Adams's various companies have been continually recognized as industry leaders by many national publications. Their latest *dream child* is Thrive Partnership, launched in 2006 to help entrepreneurs **innovate, focus** and **transform** their business to the next level of growth and profitability.

Thrive Partnership teams with business owners to help them define their goals, clarify their vision and chart a course of action for fast results and a sustainable competitive edge. The Thrive Academy of Entrepreneurship's services include strategic planning, leadership development, process improvement, marketing strategies and facilitating a wide range of targeted mastermind groups and workshops geared towards seasoned entrepreneurs.

Prior to launching Thrive, Shane Adams spent 22 years in the construction industry as the President of Grand Floridian Builders. He launched this luxury custom homebuilding business as a start-up, and under his leadership, the company became one of America's premier custom homebuilders, with projects featured in top architectural magazines.

Lisa Adams has a background in Advanced Learning Principles and a B.A. in Education from FIU. Her success as a small business founder and owner led to her inclusion in the 2003 edition of the *Who's Who Worldwide Registry of Business Leaders*. More recently, for her work with some of the largest companies in Northern Florida, she was named the

2009 Beach Chamber of Commerce Small Business Person of the Year.

The Adamses live in Panama City Beach, Florida where they share a passion for excellence, travel and new experiences. To learn more about them, and to receive a complimentary special report and "The Thrive-onomics Index" to help you identify your best business strengths, visit www.mythrivecoach.com or call (850) 230-2756.